The Essex Air
'a service worth

Essex Air Ambulance provides ... rescue service to the people of Essex. It is not funded by the government, but is supported wholly from charitable donations. This anthology is sold on the understanding that 40% of its sales revenue will go to support the Essex Air Ambulance charity. *(For more information please read preface overleaf)*

Essex Air Ambulance, The Business Centre, Earls Colne Business Park,
Earls Colne, Colchester, CO6 2NS.
Email: info@essexairambulance.org.uk

ISBN 0-9546753-1-2

COPYRIGHT RAYLEIGH LIBRARY WRITERS' GROUP 2005

All rights reserved; no part of this publication may be reproduced or transmitted by any means, electronic, mechanical, photocopied, recorded on any information storage or retrieval system without prior permission in writing from the publisher.

**First published in Great Britain 2005
By Rayleigh Library Writers' Group Press
7 Durham Way, Rayleigh Essex, SS6 9RY, England**

*Cover design and typesetting by G Harris
Artwork by Ron McEwen
Edited by Jane Hare*

Web Site: writinggroups.co.uk

Printed by Basildon Printing Company Ltd, Fleet House, Armstrong Road, Benfleet, Essex, SS7 4FH, England

In the search for a local charity for the anthology to support, the Writers decided to look no further than The Essex Air Ambulance. A localised charity run by Essex people, benefiting Essex people, and costing in excess of £100,000 a month to run, we think its services deserve both wider acclaim and wider support. Employing only nine full time staff and, despite its links with the NHS, receiving nothing from the government or, for that matter, the National Lottery, the service relies solely on the generosity of the people of Essex.

Fundraising was begun in 1997, and Lord Braybrooke, the then Lord Lieutenant of Essex, launched the service just a year later from New Hall School in Boreham. Since July 1999 it has run a seven-day daylight service, and since its inception has, up until June this year, flown over 6000 missions.

The helicopter, a fully fitted Eurocopter EC135 T2, with its crew of a pilot and two paramedics, carries full life support medical equipment and attends between three and five incidents a day. Unaffected by road congestion or tides, it is usually in the air within two minutes of an emergency call being received. No matter how inaccessible an area is to land vehicles, the helicopter is very seldom deterred from landing and is never more than eight minutes flying time from the nearest hospital.

So this Christmas it will be possible to sit by the fire and enjoy a good story, in the comfortable assurance that without the help of thousands of Essex people, like you, that helicopter whirring overhead, possibly saving a Christmas tragedy, could never have lifted from the pad. The Rayleigh Library Writers' Group feel it is an honour to be part of the fund raising organisation that helps keep the Essex Air Ambulance service in the air, and by purchasing this anthology, you have contributed to this very valuable service. Thank you from them and us.

Ken Westell

Writers' Reign
Volume II

Off the back of our success at gaining a first prize at the David St. John Thomas Charitable Trust 2005 Writing Competition with volume I of the Writers' Reign, we bring you volume II. A collection of very different short stories, comical verse and poetry from some of Essex's published and unpublished writers - and like all projects of this nature, teamwork and a sprinkling of fun is the key to success and without the effort and determination of all the members of the group, this volume would not have been possible, so thanks to everyone involved from its concept to completion.

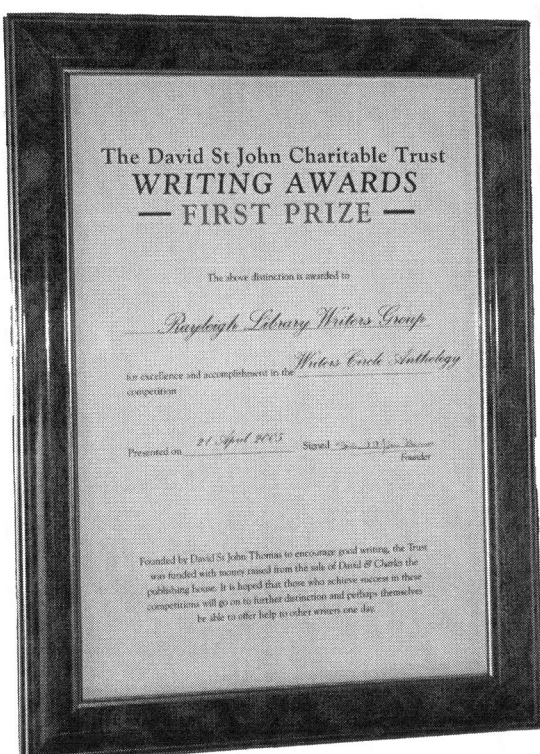

And finally not forgetting once again a special thanks to Simon Brady (Service Manager) for his contribution and to all his staff at The Rayleigh Library for putting up with us, Thanks.

Contents	Author		Page
The Coal Cellar	George Thornhill		1
Bill Who	Richard Banks	(Mini epic)	10
Bed and Breakfast	Peter Freeman		11
Funeral Blues	Amanda Gooden		18
Mr President	Peter Freeman	Limerick	22
Zorba's Dance	*Myra Baxter*	*Poetry*	23
A Devonian Tale	Keidrin Seaton		24
The Macdonald Indemnity	Ken Westell		27
Listening	*S J Banham*	*Poetry*	31
Woman	*Myra Baxter*	*Poetry*	32
Journey to the End of the Rainbow	Rosemary Clarke		33
Life is a Lottery	Doug Fraser		39
The Life and Soul of the party	*Natalie Hudson*	*Poetry*	44
Sid the Sad Spook	G K Harris	Children	45
The Homecoming	Richard Banks		50
Tony Blair	Peter Freeman	Limerick	53
The Old Sycamore Tree	*Sis Unsworth*	*Poetry*	54
Traffic	Richard Banks	(Mini epic)	54
Hotel Paradiso	Bernice Bedford		55
Purr - fect Pet	*S J Banham*	*Poetry*	58
Villeggiatura in Valdinievole	Charles Joseph	(Travel article)	59
Greed	*Natalie Hudson*	*Poetry*	64
By The Sea shore	Gwenda Syratt		65
Abandoned	Amanda Gooden	(Mini epic)	69
The Unattainable	*Natalie Hudson*	*Poetry*	70
George and the Giant	Bob French		71
Murder	Amanda Gooden		78
Getting Published	Bernice Bedford		79

Continued

A Cautionary Tale	*Natalie Hudson*	*Poetry*	*81*
Sordid Soap	**S J Banham**		**82**
The Spring of '45	*Sis Unsworth*	*Poetry*	*87*
A Model Son	**G K Harris**		**88**
Melanie	*Peter Freeman*	*Poetry*	*92*
I want to Look into your eyes	*Natalie Hudson*	*Poetry*	*93*
Fly on a diet	**Bernice Bedford**		**94**
The Queue	**Sis Unsworth and Peter Freeman**		**96**
Ghosts Versus Goolies	*Myra Baxter*	*Poetry*	*100*
The Meaning of Us	*Natalie Hudson*	*Poetry*	*101*
Out There	*Myra Baxter*	*Poetry*	*102*

The Coal Cellar
by George Thornhill

Monday morning had cracked open cold and misty. The long, hot summer days of climbing shady trees in an Islington park and skimming stones across the murky water of the canal now a fading memory, as the falling leaves of autumn beckoned finger-like to the icy wraiths of winter.

The weekend had clattered past far too quickly. Saturday morning pictures, with a fourpenny Jubbly to drink and a hand full of Blackjacks to chew while Flash Gordon saved the universe, then the dash home with scores of other children across the bombed site, fighting the kids that lived in the flats.

Sunday morning awoke to the chorus of church bells. The street outside was silent: empty. There was no traffic; no whirr of a starter motor and the reluctant cough from an exhaust pipe as a cold engine shuddered into life. No one in the street owned a car, so the sound of the bells rang as sharp as crystal. I counted at least five different peels, some near and some far away.

Dad always cleaned the two sash windows in the bedroom at the front of the house if it wasn't raining. He would sit with his bottom parked out of the building on the windowsill, while his legs dangled into the bedroom, then he would pull the sash down onto his lap and clean the outside of the panes of glass with a yellow duster and some pink cleaning liquid. I thought my dad was very brave, sitting on the windowsill the way he did.

The Coal Cellar

Our two rooms were on the first floor of a terraced house and it was a long drop down to the basement area and the coal cellar. A dark spidery place that lay unseen, hidden beneath the pavement.

Sunday lunch was roast beef and Yorkshire pudding while Family Favourites played on the radiogram, then out to play in the backyard until tea and then bed.

I hated bedtime. During the summer, I couldn't understand why I had to go to bed when it was still daylight outside and in the winter it was dark and frightening. The one dim light bulb that hung precariously from two frayed wires in the middle of the room was always turned off, plunging my small world into the nightmare realm of the nocturnal creatures, goblins and the bogeyman. There was a lamppost outside in the street and stray light cast shadows from the glazing bars onto the curtains. The thin yellow drapes moved now and again, ruffled by cold draughts of air blowing in round gaps in the window frame and the shadows danced angrily on the outside of the curtains as if trying to get into the room.

Sometimes I used to hear noises and would bang on the wall for someone to come. I knew that I would be shouted at and told to stop being silly, but it would be worth it just to have the bedroom door open for a few minutes to let the light in. My mother would sit on my bed and pull the handkerchief from the top pocket of my pyjamas for me to wipe away the tears, while threatening me with my father's wrath if I didn't be quiet and go to sleep.

Once I saw a mouse run from under my bed. My mother didn't see it; it scampered across my bedside mat and disappeared down a hole in the floorboards. I tried to tell her, but I was sobbing too much and the words got stuck between gasps of breath and wouldn't come out.

But now the demons of the night had passed with the dawn and I hurried to get dressed. It was freezing.

I heard my mum getting breakfast ready across the landing in the other room that made up our home. Dad was already at work, having been woken at five in the morning by the man with the long wooden pole tapping on the window from the street, calling my father for his shift at the factory.

Then after breakfast it was off to school. I didn't like school much; the corridors were tiled black and white and smelled strongly of disinfectant. Miss Stamp, our teacher, would make us chant our seven times table, standing up at our wooden desks while she clapped her hands together in time to our mathematical rhythm. But today I didn't mind. Today was special as the coalman was going to deliver coal and there would be a fire in the kitchen-come-living room, but not the bedroom. That only happened if you were ill and the doctor called.

Mum would buy a bundle of firewood kindling from the ironmonger's shop round the corner and make up the fire with screwed up balls of newspaper. Then came the magic moment when she struck the match and the hearth crackled into life.

An open fire wasn't just for warmth it meant that the winter season had started. The hopscotch numbers and 'whirlies' chalked onto the pavement would be washed away in the rain and replaced with marbles in the playground. An open fire meant warm hands after a snowball fight: hot buttered toast and crumpets on Sunday afternoon. An open fire, like the smell of celery in the greengrocer's, meant that Christmas was just round the corner.

"I bet he's already gone," whispered David, as we stood behind our chairs put up on our desks, waiting for the final bell.

"Who?"

"The coalman."

David was my friend and lived with his family in the two rooms below us on the ground floor; his dad was a lorry driver.

It was David who first told me about the dragons that lived in the fire. He reckoned that the mother dragons used to lay their eggs in the coalmines. You couldn't see the eggs, of course, because they were invisible. But they needed the heat from the fire to hatch, and if you were lucky you could see the baby dragons crawling about in the hot embers before they flew up the chimney in a wisp of orange flame and blue smoke.

The run home from the school gates turned into a race between me and a dozen other children, and as we turned the corner by the bakers, the coalman's dray was in our street. It had four wooden wheels with iron tyres and the flat bed was half full with sacks of coal stacked upright one behind the other. The children surrounded the front of the horse, patting its neck and stroking its ears, while the animal had its head buried in a sack of oats suspended from its neck. David, on the other hand, stood at the rear of the horse, watching in case it lifted its tail and made a deposit on the road. David was funny like that. He was the only kid I knew that wasn't frightened of the dark. My mum reckoned he was fey; whatever that meant.

The coalman was a burly figure with ruddy red cheeks and a ginger moustache speckled with coal dust and was always happy to chat with us kids, although he never allowed any of us to ride on his dray. He wore a waistcoat, hobnailed boots and a round leather skullcap with a leather flap that hung down the back to protect his neck.

He always worked quickly, lifting the round iron lids in the middle of the pavement that covered the manholes into the cellar, then in one practiced movement, he lifted a sack full of coal onto his back and up-ended it over his shoulder into the manhole, kicking any stray black lumps with his boot before moving the horse onto the next one.

The houses in our street were three storeys high from the pavement, plus a basement and a coal cellar; one outside scullery for doing the washing and one inside toilet that was shared among the families that lived in the building. A common staircase ran up all the way through the house from the yard at the back to the top floor, with two rooms per family spaced across an open landing.

In our house, the two rooms in the basement were empty. It was a dark place full of cobwebs where the bogeyman lived. I was too frightened to go down to the toilet at night and used the potty under my bed.

"Come on," shouted a voice from the pavement. "Let's go and see the coal drop down the hole in number 11."

Half a dozen kids flew along the passage and down the dark staircase to the basement. I didn't mind going down there at that time of day as there was still enough light filtering through the grime-covered windows to see and, besides, I wasn't alone.

A cone of light shot into the coal cellar like the beam from Buck Rogers' space ship as the coalman lifted the cover. Then came the coal. A cheer went up as one bag after another fell from the street until there was a heap of coal that was taller than me. Then the inky blackness returned as the coalman replaced the iron lid over the hole in the pavement.

"I'm going to be king of the castle," I said, climbing up the heap.

"You'll be in trouble with your mum if you get dirty," retorted Ann from over the road, whose white ankle socks were covered in coal dust. I trod carefully making sure my foothold was sound before moving up and then I was there, standing on top of the coal heap.

"Come on, let's go," said a spectator, trying to make little of my achievement.

"Wait for me."

But they didn't and by the time I had scrambled back down they were gone. I called up from the basement area just as the other kids ran out of the front door above me into the street. I shouted after them again, but all that greeted my calls were the fading voices of my friends, like the sound of a train speeding away into the distance and then silence.

I started to feel uneasy. Had it really just got darker all of a sudden? I'm sure it was lighter when we came down.

I stood at the entrance to the basement room and looked across to where I knew the door should be, but I couldn't see it and couldn't remember whether it was open or closed when we came through. Perhaps I should run across the room? But what if the door was stuck and I couldn't get it open? I shrank back two paces into the area. The fading daylight offered little comfort.

I looked upwards forlornly to the street above hoping to see someone there when I noticed the drainpipe running up the wall. I had managed to climb it once on a hot sunny day when my fingers got a good grip on the pipe, but it had started to rain and I knew the pipe would be wet and slippery.

I heard a noise from inside the basement and I froze in terror. My breathing had stopped: my heart started to thump and my ears strained to listen for the slightest sound, too scared to think what monster might be waiting for me in the darkness. Did the bogeyman really eat children?

The floorboards creaked. I definitely heard it and then they creaked again and I felt my knees turn to jelly.

"W...Who's there?"

For a moment, I thought I saw a shadow inside pass by the window. Then, the floorboards creaked again.

"Is that you David?" I called, knowing how he always liked to play tricks.

"Yea, it's only me, did I scare you?"

A sense of relief flooded through my body from the neck down, and I felt my fingertips itch.

"For a minute I thought you was the bogeyman."

"The bogeyman," replied David laughing. "You mean One-Eye Murphy?"

"I've never heard him called Murphy before, is that his real name?"

David's voice sounded odd, talking with the same Irish accent as his mum. He often did that, trying to make out that he was somebody else.

"So how did he lose his eye then?" I asked trying to catch him out.

"He said he lost it at Waterloo."

"How the hell did he lose his eye at a railway station?"

"I don't know, he told me a Frenchman did it to 'im," said David.

"Why don't you come in to the room, we could play a game?"

David was cunning; he had caught me before like this. Either he had a spud gun or a water pistol and was just waiting for the chance to get me back after I burst a paper bag on his head the other day.

"What game should we play?" I asked.

"I could show you my drum, it belongs to Murphy really but he lets me play it. I'll let you have a go."

"You haven't got a drum, not a real one," I insisted. "Only your sister's toy drum and that doesn't count."

"Yes I have, you listen."

David's voice bristled with confidence. I heard the sound of something hollow scrape along the floorboards and the click of two pieces of wood banging together, then the brat-tat-tat, brat-tat-tat of a drum. The sound echoed round the basement as David continued to play, and I was half tempted to enter the room to see how he was performing this trick. It sounded like a real drum, but then David was clever, and I remembered how good a shot he was with the spud gun.

"My mum will be here in a minute to fetch the coal," I shouted above the din. "And besides, it's nearly time for tea, and I'm starving."

The drumming stopped.

"I haven't eaten for a hundred years," said David. "I've forgotten what food tastes like."

"Know what you mean," I replied, feeling my stomach gurgle.

I started to wipe the drizzle from the back of the drainpipe with my coat sleeve when I heard another noise from inside the basement, but this time it was mum with the coalscuttle and a clip round the ear, no doubt, if she'd thought I'd been climbing up the coal heap. There was nothing for it, I had to shin up the drainpipe.

Putting my hands behind the pipe, I braced my feet against the wall and pushed, climbing as fast as I could. I'd reached the railings by the time my mum walked across the area to the coal cellar; she was wearing her pinafore and scarf and luckily for me, she didn't look up. Then one more effort and I clambered over the railings onto the front door step.

"Did you see David in the basement Mum?" I called as she came back through a few seconds later.

"Oh there you are," she said. "No, there's no one down here; come and get washed up for tea."

"I'm right here," said a familiar voice.

I spun round to come face to face with David. The front door was pulled to, so he couldn't have walked past me, and it would have taken him ages to climb over the back wall into the next yard and come up into the street from number 13.

"How did you get out of the basement so quickly?"

"I wasn't down in the basement," replied David with a triumphant smile on his face. "I was watching the coalman's horse. It lifted its tail and plopped onto the road near the school gates. I saw the coalman shovel it into his bucket."

Later that night, I lay alone in my bedroom surrounded by darkness. I was too scared to breathe properly in case there was something in the room that saw me move. I took sharp shallow breathes through my mouth; clenching the eiderdown with my fists; pulling it tight against my nose. Then, I heard a noise. I felt the tears well up inside and tried to fight back the sobbing that was making my chest bounce under the bedclothes.

I heard it again, but this time the sound was unmistakable. It was the brat-tat-tat of a drum. I pressed my ear to the pillow but the noise didn't seem to be coming from under my bed like it usually did, it was coming from outside.

Gathering all my courage, I tiptoed quietly across the floorboards to the window. I drew back the curtains and saw my friend David from downstairs standing out in the street in his pyjamas and bare feet, waving.

The brat-tat-tat of the drum was getting louder, then, as if walking through a fog, a troop of soldiers wearing redcoats, black hats and long knee-length boots that crunched in the road gravel, came marching down the street. Each soldier carried a long musket over his shoulder and marched in time. Left right, left right.

Leading the soldiers, was a boy that looked to be about twelve years old and it was he that carried the drum. He wore the same uniform as the soldiers, but had a black patch over one eye.

Marching next to him, was another boy about the same age, but he was dressed in a waistcoat, flat cap and wore a red scarf round his neck. He waved to David on the doorstep, then, he looked up at the window, smiled and waved at me. I felt butterflies in my tummy and I waved back as hard as I could. They marched to the end of the street, then disappeared into the fog; brat-tat-tat, brat-tat-tat.

David was gone when I looked down at the front door step and I stood there for a few minutes longer, hoping the soldiers would march down the street again; but they didn't, so I tiptoed back to my bed. As I lay there, I made up my mind that tomorrow night, before it got too dark, I would go down to the coal cellar. Alone.

Bill Who?

Bill was a sullen, brooding brute of a man - a product of the London slums. He had endured desperate poverty and squalor and somehow survived into manhood. Now it was him against the world. He would crack heads, rob houses, do anything rather than go hungry or accept the grim charity of the workhouse. For him there were no friends - just the wary allegiance of fellow thieves, a wretched dog on which he vented his frustration and the unrepricated devotion of a prostitute he was later to murder.

by Richard Banks

Bed and Breakfast
by Peter Freeman

"Hello! I'm Norman Plant," said I firmly, trying to look important but at the same time friendly and approachable.

"I thought you might be… and about time too!" said the nice lady,

"I'm going out tonight and I've been sat here in me frock for the last hour!"

At this I attempted to soothe her by praising her hairdo and fetching attire but she, no doubt intent on casting aside her domestic shackles for a Saturday night knees up, would have none of it and continued;

"I can't stop now. Have you eaten?"

"No I jus…"

"Well you'd better bring your things in and get down the pub."

"Here's the key to this; and here's the key to that; no pets; no smoking; do do this; and don't do that; there's a list in the room. I'm off out; see you in the morning. Bye."

With that, the 'Nice Lady' was gone, leaving only her fragrance and, like the 'Cheshire Cat', her smile, which remained long after the rest of her had departed.

That day was concluded with a good pub meal and a pot or two of real ale to wash it down. The memory of how I got to bed is somewhat blurred but I can vaguely recall a very narrow room and blundering about in the dark.

Morning announced itself with watery sun so I arose, stepping into a puddle of cold liquid which was lying in wait for me beside the bed. This, I was sure, must in some way be my fault so the next hour or so was spent mopping it up with anything I could find.

Next I squeezed myself hopefully into the tiny shower cubical provided and gingerly turned on the tap. I was rewarded with a less than enthusiastic flow of tepid rust coloured water; this being accompanied by the most frightening crashes and bangs from the water pipes that I have ever heard. It was like the London blitz!

Once jammed into the overgrown sardine tin, I found that there was only enough room to stand; any attempt to wash or even raise ones' arms, was out of the question.

Meanwhile, secreted in its cobwebbed lair, the boiler, like some monstrous demented octopus, in its rage dispatched its thunder demons through copper tentacles to every far corner of its empire. All about me, from every part of the house, I could hear them rehearsing the end of the world with total abandon.

Not to be outdone I defiantly joined in with my own operatic rendering and so starred in the very first performance of Concerto No.1 in B flat minor (for abused plumbing and naked fat man) ever to be heard in the county of Shropshire.

The contortions needed to extricate myself from the cold and steely embrace of that shower unit have no place in these pages gentle reader, since this account may fall into the hands of children or those of a delicate disposition.

Thus having made the best of it, shaved and combed the rust from my hair, I sat down on the bed and, serenaded by the continued, though diminishing music of the pipes, planned my next move.

The notice board informed me that breakfast would be delivered to my room at 8.30, so having carefully removed the folding table from its wall clips, I competently assembled it and placed my finished masterpiece in the only available space - in front of the bedroom door

Mopping up the blood from my shredded fingers took but a moment, and once I had located the plastic chair I was able to take my lordly ease and look about me.

At the far end of the room, I noticed, lived a small bedside cabinet. On this there stood a battered alarm clock; three square upon its little round legs. It had the look of one that had seen a thousand dramas and kept a thousand secrets.

This clock had obviously been the victim of much ill treatment; no doubt forced upon it by those intent on making it talk, and also, perversely, by those that would have it be silent. Upon its head, it wore as in the office of a hat, a dented bell; which, no doubt due to frequent and violent contact with the wall, had become somewhat tilted giving it a brisk and jaunty air. It reminded me of the French sailor who had cheekily pinched the bum of my lady companion one rainy morning in Dieppe, in the days when we still had proper steam trains.

Instantly I recognised a cheerful and valiant comrade in that battered timepiece and no longer felt alone. That stalwart clock, without fear or favour was prepared to serve prince or pauper with equal dedication. It just got on with things and played the hand dealt to it without complaint. I can still bring it to mind when things are going badly and it never fails to put the bones back in my corset.

At this point there came a soft rap on the door and the voice of an angel cried "Breakfast!"

No doubt you will have noticed the very understandable error in my thinking gentle reader: the fly in my soup, the death watch beetle in my attic, the barricaded door in my breakfast delivery arrangements.

Imagine my plight. Here was I trapped, imprisoned like Mrs Rochester behind my bedroom door. Whilst only feet away the 'Nice Lady,' no doubt still smiling and still in her nightie, was waiting to give me her tasty offering. Food that she had carefully and lovingly selected and prepared with her own soft hands.

I began wrenching at the door in a masterful way in a vain attempt to create a gap big enough to admit a large horizontal dinner plate. Some precious moments were wasted at this enterprise before the 'Nice Lady,' no doubt guided by previous experience, intoned in a slightly exasperated voice:

"You'll 'ave to lift it up else we could be 'ere all morning."

The intended significance of this advice did not at first impinge itself upon my brain cell since it had now gone off in a fantasy all its own (the details of which may be found in a separate publication which, if requested, will be sent to your home in a brown paper wrapper).

It was the table you see, it was the table. She wanted me to lift up the table in order to open the door a little wider.

Stung into action, I quickly grasped one of its scrawny legs and raised it as far as the low ceiling and the shower cubical would permit; thus allowing just enough room for a manicured hand to pass my breakfast plate around the edge of the door. Pressure off, the door closed once more leaving the table free to get itself tangled up in the clips intended for its stowage.

With my background of advanced engineering and Lego, I quickly realised that two hands would be required to rectify matters and that one of mine was holding a plate. Gingerly I tried to release my grip on the table so that I could dash off and find somewhere safe to leave my breakfast. The table however forestalled this plan by threatening to wrench out its clips and plunge to the floor in a tangle of recriminations and broken legs. After struggling for some time and without quite knowing how, I managed to swap hands; which at first I thought merely left me with a mirror image of the original problem. A more thorough investigation of this new state however revealed that by stretching into the extreme distance and using the very tips of my fingers, I could now manage to balance the breakfast plate on the rim of my tiny hand basin.

This done I then gave my full attention to the table, which knew when it was beaten and gave up without further resistance. Having set out my knife and fork and arranged the condiments in a pleasing pattern, I turned again to the plate…
(Yes?.............No it hadn't fallen onto the carpet and landed food side down!)

If it had have been a good, manly, wholesome, breakfast, well endowed with baked beans, black puddings and greasy bits, then I'm sure, that like any self respecting breakfast, it would have taken great joy in falling to the floor in exactly that manner.

This breakfast however was a very different beast. This breakfast was a survivor; lean and mean, it had street cred, it had seen a bit of life. For a start its plate was cold; none of your dissolute namby pamby warmed up plates for this breakfast. Its one egg, fried for twenty minutes and left for an hour to congeal, looked as if it had been provided by a miserly crow. It had the taste and feel of solidified latex. I have never tried to eat Tupperware but now feel that I am well prepared for such a venture.

The bacon provided was the only member of the gang to display any decency at all and had very laudably curled itself up out of shame. Despite that however, deep down, it was no different from the rest. No doubt corrupted by the egg and the single burned and scrawny sausage, it tasted like old leather.

I did not get to taste that sausage - perhaps I was spared - for my enthusiastic attempt to decapitate it with the blunt knife provided was enough to cause it to jump from my plate and hide under the bed.

Chewing what was left of the meal proved to be a long and arduous task with no pleasure in it. During this exercise it came to my mind that the knife had most likely been deliberately blunted to prevent paying customers from cutting their own wrists before settling the bill.

Seeking to assist my agonised chewing, I conceived the notion of making myself another mug of tea and in pursuit of this enterprise, diligently inspected the water level in the kettle. It was low, too low; its little element was exposed. (Ah!)

Clearly more water was required and the only source that appeared to be drinkable was the cold tap of the small hand basin.

Therein lay another problem however since the kettle could not easily be presented to the tap. I tried various alignments before finally discovering the trick of it. There was only one possible way that the kettle could be sited successfully within that basin and only I could have found it.

The tap I discovered was a passionate all or nothing affair and once turned on, would insist on giving its all when a more restrained response would have been quite sufficient. It was in fact, like trying to catch the Niagara Falls in a bucket.

For a moment, transfixed by horror, I watched the torrent of water enter the kettle; pause for an instant, gather itself and then rush up the spout and describe a perfect arc in its familiar journey across the room, landing precisely and with clinical accuracy, on the wet patch in front of the bedside cabinet. Turning off the tap took but a moment and I was then left with just enough water in the kettle to make two mugs of tea: and just enough water under the bed to float a Cross-Channel Ferry.

It came to mind that should the 'Nice Lady' inquire as to what that sausage was doing under the bed, I could now reply with the old chestnut "the breast stroke most likely!" And be forgiven by my peers.

When at last I got around to the one slice of toast and scraped the burned bits from both sides, I could see light through it and found that it would burst into crumbs, if any attempt was made to spread it with marmalade.

Around about this time I began to feel that the rest of my life was beckoning and that room two would have to manage without me.

Soon I had: stepped in the wet patch again, donned my last pair of dry socks, packed my bag and returned the furniture to its lodgings.

As I turned to go I gave the room that had been my shelter, my prison and my torture chamber for the past eight hours or so, one final glance, and my eye lit upon the battered alarm clock. It had assumed a slightly forlorn look, and the final picture in my mind is of that most resolute of companions standing bravely to attention on its little cabinet, rakish bell at just the right angle and its little hands spread wide as if in supplication at precisely 9.15. As I closed the door for the last time the conviction came to me that that clock needed a more stable existence; someone to be there for it on a more permanent basis, not just a parade of passing strangers: but then don't we all?

Funeral Blues
by Amanda Gooden

My brother David always said that I'd be late for my own funeral - and I very nearly was! I managed to sneak in through the open door of the chapel just as it slammed shut, nearly trapping the hem of Auntie Vera's best black coat. She wore that for my wedding as well - she never did like me very much. I suppose you're thinking that I didn't have to use the door like everyone else, that I could easily have walked straight through it like any self-respecting ghost. Give me a chance; I've only been dead a week!

I noticed a strange, heavy atmosphere inside the chapel that was typical of such occasions. I managed a quick head count as everyone settled in their seats. Eighty five mourners, give or take a few; most in black, but mad Uncle Arnold wearing his customary red anorak. I'd seen Auntie Vera shouting at him outside, but she should have left him alone; Arnold always did his own thing, everyone understood him. Why should things be any different now?

The vicar had an egg yolk stain on the back of his cassock. I bet he thought no-one would notice. But I noticed. When my brother went up to read the eulogy, the vicar turned sideways - I bet he thought he'd covered all his bases and no-one would be any the wiser.

There were a few sobs as my brother read of my life, my

collection of bus tickets and my job at the local undertakers. Everyone laughed when I started there, but I got a free funeral out of it, so who's laughing now, eh'?

His speech was written in longhand on a piece of lined A4 paper torn out of my nephew Michael's history folder. I was his only sister; you think he'd have made more of an effort. He'd somehow managed to screw it up into a ball in the pocket of his suit jacket, so he had to iron it flat with the palm of his hand before starting. Typical David - no planning, no preparation, just 'making do'.

My best friend Annie was sitting one row back from the front, staring down at half a packet of Kleenex that she'd managed to shred between her fingers. I saw that she was wearing the blouse that she'd borrowed from me last summer. It fitted her better so I said she could keep it. I wish I hadn't now. It had been pure white, but she'd obviously washed it in with the 'coloureds' so now it had a strange blueish tinge to it - particularly at the collar. She never took care of anything. I ought to pay her a visit at home in the next week or so, reorganise her washing basket. I think she'd like that.

On the same row as Annie but over near the window was a boy I went to school with. He was a man now, of course, but I hadn't clapped eyes on him since we left school nearly 30 years ago last June. I couldn't even remember his name and yet there he was, not only at my funeral, but crying and having the nerve to sit one row back from the front! The cheek of it!

'One row back from the front' is for family and close friends, everyone knows that. And if there's no-one close enough to sit there, then you leave a gap, in case they turn up late. That's etiquette. But no, there was Russell, Rodney, Raymond, whatever his bloomin' name was, bold as brass, sitting in the seat that, by rights, my second cousin Dawn should have had. And you could tell by the look on Dawn's face that she wasn't impressed. She'd evidently put a lot of thought into her outfit, had Dawn; matching shoes and handbag, the lot. And she wasn't happy when it all went to waste in a seat behind a pillar at the back of the chapel. It's not like a wedding, where you get to be in the photos, oh no. Dawn's moment of colour co-ordination was destined to be lost to the world forever. It's a good job I could see it all.

Dawn was with her husband Terry. You know Terry - tall, red face, silver rimmed glasses, gormless looking. That's the one. He'd made an effort, clothes-wise, as well. Or rather Dawn had made an effort on his behalf. I'd seen her make him spit on a handkerchief so she could wipe his face before they got out of their Ford Escort in the crematorium car park. Dawn had always treated Terry like a child and everyone in the family felt sorry for him. She was loud and bossy, a real 'Hyacinth Bucket' character. I liked her though. Say what you like about Dawn, but all her family had clean faces.

I remember looking down on the congregation from somewhere up near the ceiling of the chapel. Somewhere you don't usually get to go. Where, evidently, the cleaners never went, either. There were cobwebs galore draped over everything and dust as far as the eye could see. There was a stained glass window on the north side of the chapel that sparkled in the sunlight, but was actually filthy up close. I resisted the urge to write my name in the dirt.

My investigation into the general hygiene levels in the chapel meant that I missed the bulk of what David had to say but caught a bit of the vicar's waffling. "Pillar of the community, blah blah blah, charity work, blah blah blah, a loyal and trusted friend, blah blah blah…" Was that me he was talking about? The only charity work I've ever done was a sponsored walk at school in aid of the local dog's home, and I was made to do that. Hardly makes me Mother Teresa, does it?

I floated back down to ground level, vowing to bring a duster and some Windolene with me on my next visit. There wasn't a dry eye in the house as my coffin disappeared behind the moving curtain to the strains of 'Somewhere Over the Rainbow'. I wanted 'Disco Inferno' but my nearest and dearest had always told me that wouldn't happen - it was in 'bad taste', apparently. But whose funeral was this exactly? I also wanted a curtain call and an encore, but it wasn't to be either.

Everyone filtered outside, shaking hands with the vicar - the egg stain looked even worse up close. They all said the same thing, "Thank you, lovely service". Uncle Arthur studied a painting of some trees on his way out in a valiant attempt to avoid the collection plate. It worked, as well - one up to Uncle Arthur!

Outside, everyone did their level best to try and get a glimpse of their own floral tribute, to see if theirs was the biggest. Human nature I suppose, but the collection of baskets, sprays and dodgy shaped wreaths were supposed to be there in my memory, not for a display of one-upmanship. I watched as they all drifted off into a collection of cars and taxis and disappeared out of the gates of the crematorium on their way to 'The Dog and Duck' to eat their own weight in sausage rolls.

And that was that. I was tempted to follow, to see what wonderful stories they would all recall or invent at the wake, but decided against it. I had other things to do now, other places to visit. At the end of the day, if you can go anywhere you want, a lunchtime funeral buffet at the dusty 'Dog and Duck' somehow loses its appeal.

You can tell a lot about a person by their funeral, apparently, or so Auntie Mavis used to say. So what, exactly, will she make of 47 floral tributes and 3 different fillings in the vol-au-vents? I bet she's impressed. She wandered from table to table at my wedding, totally plastered with her hat on back to front proudly proclaiming, "I'm the Auntie, you know" to anyone who would listen.

Give it an hour or two, she'll be doing the same thing today, sherry in hand. Everyone will smile, Auntie Vera will roll her eyes and Robert, Raymond or whatever his name is will have to give her a lift home in his car after she misses the last bus.

And that's how it should be. I am dead, I've ceased to exist, I've "shuffled off this mortal coil", never to return. But by tomorrow, my family and friends will get back to normal, start living their lives again and moaning about the cost of their council tax. And rightly so - it's all a rip off.

And what will I do? Well, I have plenty to keep me busy. I'm going to meet Elvis, for a start, ask him why he ever thought that white rhinestone-studded jumpsuits were the wisest choice for man with an expanding waistline. I'm going to do a parachute jump; nothing to worry about now I'm dead, what can go wrong? And I'm going to gradually, in time, do all the things that I wouldn't do, all the things I couldn't do, was too scared to do, couldn't afford to do, never had the time to do. I'm going to live death to the full. And I'm going to start by giving the stained glass window in the chapel a good going over with hot soapy water…

**A lass with a beautiful smile
the president tried to beguile.
In order to please,
she went down on her knees
and his details came out (at the trial).
Peter Freeman**

Zorba's Dance

The click of his fingers glide, dip and prance
Zorba once more on the wings of his dance

Whatever life throws he can take it now
To none of life's problems will he bow

Arms outstretched, his spirit soars high
Embracing Earth, Sea and Sky

Life can be hard when dreams lie in tatters
But keep keeping on, that is what matters

When he dances, head raised to the skies
All life is mirrored in Zorba's eyes

His dance tells of feelings, body and soul
Some madness it takes to make a man whole

This his philosophy bears him along
Who dares to say if he's right or wrong

When we express in the manner we choose
Then we join Zorba in our dancing shoes

by Myra Baxter

A DEVONIAN TALE
by Keidrin Seaton

Have you ever had that experience when you see something from the corner of your eye but then, when you turn to look at it, it isn't there?

I'd spent the whole afternoon, sitting on the bedroom floor, sorting through the stuff in some cardboard boxes. They were stuffed with the sort of detritus one accumulates over the years, kept "just in case..." It was late October, and I'd shut the door to keep in what little warmth a watery Dartmoor sun had been delivering to the room.

Well, as I say, I'd sat there all afternoon and as I worked I'd looked up once or twice because from the corner of my eye I thought my cat, Pashte, was curled up asleep on the end of the bed... only she wasn't. Eventually mogshade was approaching. (It's a lovely word, isn't it? It's very ancient; it means "twilight" and it somehow seemed so appropriate for that time of day up there on the moors.) Anyway, I decided it was high time Pashte came in, so I went to look for her, closing the bedroom door behind me to keep in the warmth.

I didn't bother with a coat - I wouldn't be long - and closing the front door, I crunched across the gravel of the front yard, clicking on my powerful Halogen torch as I turned onto the lane. I glanced to the left where the road descended steeply between high granite hedge-banks that separated it from the sloping fields, but I turned to the right. In that direction the road levelled out, and, opposite the bungalow's frontage and adjacent woodland, there was the lightly wooded area that I knew to be Pashte's favourite haunt.

It was still light enough to see without the torch, but I thought if Pashte were playing hard-to-find her eyes might catch its light. Besides, there was this odd stretch of perhaps thirty yards that appeared impervious to light at any time, day or night. I'd noticed car headlights behaved as if confronted with a wall of fog there - except their light seemed somehow to be swallowed up, absorbed rather than bounced back. I guessed it was probably due to a slight dip in the road there, and the torch, being more manoeuvrable, would solve the problem. Actually, it didn't; in fact even in the half light, the beam of the torch, which boasted a quarter-mile range, made no impression; the beam simply didn't penetrate. Come to think of it, it's a funny thing: it was at that same place where the horses always shied, and also it must be about on a level with the dark patch that I found some odd rock formations in the woods on either side of the road, though whether or not they were man-made I couldn't tell you. Anyway, I have to say, none of this crossed my mind at the time. My only concern was for my absent moggie.

"I'll go to the bend in the road", I thought. "She won't have gone further than that." I strolled on, calling Pashte as I went, but there was no response. I'd gone perhaps thirty yards - just beyond the 'dark spot' - when suddenly my hackles began to rise. It felt as though eyes were boring into my back... only - you'll think I'm daft! - they weren't the eyes of anything remotely human. I froze. Now I've had some weird experiences over the years - been on ghost hunts and that sort of thing - well, I didn't have much choice, being a paranormal investigator! But nothing I'd encountered had ever scared me... until that moment. How can I describe it? The feeling was of something infinitely ancient... and infinitely malevolent.

I don't know how long I stood there. I felt, as the saying goes, rooted to the spot by sheer blind terror, icicles growing down my spine. It was probably only seconds though it felt much longer. But finally, summoning all my will, I turned and I fled.

Of course there was nothing in the lane; nothing - as far as I could see - in the woods either. No matter: I ran faster than I've ever run, back up the lane, in the gate, slamming it behind me, and in through the front door. Only then did I pause, almost sick with the exertion, to catch my breath. And only then did it dawn on me what an idiot I was. "Come on, you twerp!" I told myself. "It's not like you to be spooked like that!" Even so, it took me a few minutes to regain some semblance of composure.

And that, as they say, might very well have been that, except when I unlatched the bedroom door, still worrying over Pashte's whereabouts, and switched on the light, there she was. My pretty little cat was curled up on the end of the bed, just waking as if from a profound slumber, exactly where I'd 'seen' her earlier from the corner of my eye. Well, needless to say, I was heartily relieved but puzzled... to put it mildly!

I know what you're going to ask: but, no, there was nowhere she could have been hiding in the room when I left it. Yet as I sat down beside her and rubbed under her chin I couldn't help thinking of the time a wise friend had censured me for laughing at Lovecraft's tales of Cthulhu. And of another time when he had spoken of those ancient places, so beloved of the Celtic storytellers, where beings can pass between the worlds...

THE MACDONALD INDEMNITY
by Ken Westell

She had decided to save herself. The villagers had laughed when she told them what she had foreseen in her bluestone mirror. That in its polished obsidian surface, she had watched King George's treacherous Campbells fall on their unsuspecting MacDonald hosts. Seen those who escaped the massacre, slaughtered as they sought to hide in the hills above Glencoe Pass.

Face hidden in her plaid, she hurried along Ballachulish's single street, hard with February's frost. The sounds of drinking and card playing came from the rush dip lit cottages. Traditionally, Highland hospitality demanded visitors were made welcome.

Passing folk averted their eyes from hers. Since a small child it had been said of her that by raising her index finger, she could stop a cow's milk. This did not stop herdsmen from asking advice on a sick animal. Although still a young girl, women as far away as Lochaber relied upon her for her potions, and darker things beside.

Instinctively she cleared the village, turning her face to the wind that poured down on her. Her clairvoyant knowledge lent fear to her feet, until she topped the summit.

She stopped to catch her breath. She had walked a good three miles but such was the clarity of the Highland winter night, the lights of Ballachulish could still be faintly discerned.

Breathing deeply, concentrating, closing her eyes, she took refuge in her inner self. Her animistic instincts came fully alive; the roaring wind became her ally. Acting as a messenger, it brought the unmistakeable musky scent of deer.

Now assured and needing no light, she found what she sought. Just over the mountaintop, a small herd had found shelter in a hollow. Approaching down wind she was amongst them before they became startled. Swiftly she lay down between two hinds, soothing them with her hands and body. Making small reassuring noises deep in her throat.

Within minutes they quietened and settled once more. She felt her plaid beginning to absorb their warmth as she too collected herself for sleep.

****

The frost-saturated early morning mist wrapped the village in a white winding sheet of death. The Campbells had revelled in the butchering. Now deserted by the living, Ballachulish was a charnel house. The dead lay in all postures. Now unconcerned whether or not they met the evil eye, they stared back at her unseeingly as she walked past.

Her Clan Chief lay amongst three dead Campbells. The massive family claymore still in his blood-soaked hand. After a brief struggle she took it from his dead grasp.

Unchallenged, she walked on. The weapon, the embodiment of the Clan MacDonald, becoming an icon in her hands.
She reached the heights above the teeming narrows where the river met Loch Leven.

She heard a small clear voice, and knew why she had been born with the gift. Whirling like a dervish she hurled the sword in a glittering arc into the water below.

The wind carried her prophecy to the Highlands, "As long as this sword lies undisturbed by the hand of man, no warrior from this village will ever again die in battle".

As news of it spread, her foretelling became a recruiting banner, then a battle cry, and finally a clan talisman. She lived long enough to watch young men leaving for war kneel before the river as a natural obeisance. Some even bathed in its waters. Every man from Ballachulish returned. Scarred maybe. But alive. Slowly the legends began. Almost as famed as the prowess of her fighting men.

Poverty has always been endemic in the Highlands. Over the years it became accepted that one or two sons would leave to escape destitution. The Army became a recognised, even sought after source of food and clothing.

Scots were alongside Clive in India. Wolfe used them first to terrify, and then subdue the French at Quebec. Ballachulish men now dotted the armies of the world. They fought the Americans to a bloody standstill at Lexington. With swirling kilts and wailing pipes they were alongside Sir John Moore at Corunna. Without them Waterloo would have been a defeat. Always they returned to the village.

The tradition of the expatriate warrior continued down through the years. Ballachulish men fought for foreign masters in every corner of the known world. Victoria came to the throne and with her began the expansion of the greatest Empire the world had ever seen. In the thick of the press in a hundred small battles, the kilts and pipes advertised the presence of the Ballachulish men. Always invincible, always convinced they would return home. Always overlooked by the unseen eye and led by the unseen hand of a long dead highland woman.

The Russians were crushed in the Crimea and revenge was taken for the atrocities committed by the sepoys in Calcutta. At the battle of Omdurman the Mahdi and his dervishes called them the devils in skirts, and the Boers ran before their bayonets at Magafontien.

In 1914 came the greatest sacrifice of all. Men, the villagers amongst them, left the Highlands in their thousands. Responding to the call to stem the grey horde of evil that was sweeping across France.

At home the countryside was in turmoil. Factories were commissioned, barracks were built, and docks created.

Loch Leven was no exception. The narrows were scoured to provide a deeper access.

One night as a summer storm raged across the hills, a seaman dropped an object on the bar of a loch side pub and asked if he might have credit. It had been found in the bucket of a dredger. The blade had rusted to almost nothing, but the great brass basket-like hilt could not be mistaken.

The landlord, a villager who in his youth had fought both Boer and dervish, seized it with a despairing cry. Racing into the rain he hurled it with all his strength into the dark waters. As he did so the wind rose to an agonised, eldritch scream, and the night was rent with lighting.

Many people were afterwards to swear that the figure of a young girl, barefoot, and wrapped in a plaid as of old, walked past the unseeing eyes of the landlord directly into the wind whipped waters of the loch.

It was the 2nd July 1916 when the terrible news reached Ballachulish. The great offensive had begun on the Somme. The dead bodies of forty seven villagers were hung on the rusty barbed wire facing the German trenches.

They say that on a winter's night, if sitting in the right place, the cry of a highland woman keening over the body of her dead child can still be heard on the wind.

Listening

You've been speaking for an hour now,
And I've hardly managed a word,
But I couldn't make either head or tail,
Of anything I heard!

If only you'd stop talking,
If you could only silence yourself,
I'd be able to edge a word in,
And speak about myself.

Any moment you'll stop soon,
And my time to speak will come,
Words have buzzed and hung around,
And my brain and mouth are one.

You've finally stopped and the turn is mine,
I can hardly believe the surge,
But in the chaos of the hour,
My mind has lost its urge.

So instead I sit so silently,
My brain has given up,
My mind needs forty winks to cope,
But I thank God you shut up!

by S J Banham

Woman

*If you can laugh when others frown
And bounce back up when you are down*

*If you can wield the mascara wand
even though with a shaking hand*

*If you can dish the dirt with the rest
But as a friend be one of the best*

*If you can go on a shopping spree
spend lots of dosh and grin with glee*

*If in Harrods you drive sales girls to drink
pretending to choose a fabulous mink*

*If you can handle kids, dogs, cats and life
And your man is still glad you are his wife*

Then you are a woman

by Myra Baxter

Journey to the End of the Rainbow
by Rosemary Clarke

Today's the day. My pilgrimage to see someone who you could almost say created the word music, as we know it: David Bowie. If it weren't for the girl at my side I wouldn't be here. Ten years ago, a bus accident changed my life; from walking or running I went to wheelchair and then to a stick. From clear sight to partial and from clear brain to one messed up and confused. Now I see everything from the inside of a metaphorical bubble; a bubble of which I am the only inhabitant. Thank the Gods for my training as a secretarial trouble-shooter; it gives me some order to my world.

My niece Shannon flops at the side of me in the coach, her head resting on my arm, most of her shiny dark hair tied in a pink feathery band. Some of it still manages to escape, caressing her face; rebellious like its owner. Without her I would not be sitting here, can't find my way about too well now. I feel guilty and sort of crumpled in my stomach; it's okay doing things for others but when they do them for me… well - that's just me, how I am.

Biting my fingers again - when will I stop being so jittery, it's only music! I look around at the ones who are already here, all ages, all sizes, one thing in common. You can feel the excitement, hear it, and almost touch it. Many of them in their t-shirts, some in suits and I can see a group over there in crop tops - in this weather! No, not just music.

More people with backpacks and bags scramble on, chattering and waving; they've done this before. Me? I can't even believe this is happening.

November in Southend. The place hasn't woken up yet, the frost still covers the ground, glistening on the trees and pavement. For me an early Christmas present. The coach starts up, the engine throbbing in the cold to whoops of joy from the crowd; it's catching and I join in, forgetting my niece. She wakes up, yawns, re-ties her hair and pulls her rat around her - she insists her coat is more like rat skin than sheepskin, she's funny that way.

"I'm hungry. What did you get?"

Packets of cheese and onion crisps and some fruit are devoured - we'll save the rest for later. Who knows how expensive food will be when we get there.

A guy in a checked shirt, his red hair all over the place asks "You on Bowienet?" You don't notice his appearance, mind you, the grin is all. I give him my net name and tell him it's my first time.

"We'll have to look after you then." He says.

He and Shannon get chatting as though they've been lifelong friends; she does that, so friendly that everyone feels at home with her. I sit staring out of the window at the passing traffic and houses.

My last gig was a few years ago; Donington, Metallica headlining. I learnt then that you have to be there to get the feel of the place; the tribal dances, guitar music, drums throbbing on the wind, carrying to all parts of the field to say nothing of the lights. But getting wheelchairs in and out of cars in the middle of crowds isn't my step-dad's idea of fun, plus the food was expensive so no go.

Luckily Shannon's easy, she goes with the flow liking all

kinds of music, and doesn't mind accompanying me. However the three of us - her, her sister and me - weren't too keen on the mountains of Twix bars we had to consume to get enough wrappers for the tickets for this gig. No chocolate bars on this trip.

Getting out of the door at home was the hardest part, at least that's what I thought, or was it? The preparation, one thousand and one reasons thought up as to why I shouldn't go; the truth was, I was scared. I can't take on too much, and crowds scare me. Oh Hell! What have I let myself in for?

Someone moves nearer our seats starting a conversation with others about Bowie's music. Tin Machine versus Diamond Dogs, likes and dislikes; everyone seems to like most of his work but some albums cause the beginnings of heated arguments. Luckily everyone is so high no one wants to argue in any way.

I came into it by accident about five or six years ago, that is I think it was about then, I'm not great on numbers. With the head injury I found it hard to listen to anything, especially my tapes. I still do, but I had to have something other than a baking hot hot water bottle provided by my mum to forget the pain in my head. Then I found a tape that I'd bought a while before at a price cheap enough to tape over, as the wrong album was stamped onto the tape itself.

The voice was soft and calming, and more than that it was interesting. A big plus was that it was one that didn't hurt my head. He became my staple diet, and as the pain stopped me from sleeping much I got through a lot of tapes. I loved the siren effect of his voice on my mind, making me forget some of the pain. Later I wanted to know more, I read books, albeit with a white piece of paper underneath the words. Above all I wanted to see a gig; to experience what others had and be part of it all.

Bowie's stage sets are famous, beating even Metallica for

spectacle. I remember seeing a tape of a stage show that a penfriend had given me; the huge white hand, strange costumes and flashing white lights too big for a mere tape. My friend sent me lots more, some he'd taken himself, and at that time it was my only way of seeing the concerts. Some of them had huge banks of televisions on the wall allowing everyone to see him, every time different; more alluring or alarming, a chameleon if ever there was one.

I look around at the posters on some of the windows; the time of being there was drawing nearer. One of the suits, now thin on top, starts to recall memories of his first gig. A young man, cold in the middle of a field with others, waiting for an appearance from the man himself then curly haired and almost fey, the sun coming over a stage set like a pyramid and the first few strains of notes echoing on the air. The atmosphere in the coach is filled with others telling their stories, each one reliving each moment with gusto. To each teller an almost holy experience.

Basildon; an ice block in Essex even in the summer. The sun's come out now, brightening up the cold brick buildings. At each bus stop the pile of people lean on the metal bars that fence it in; their bags resting on the pull down seats along with their feet, heavy trainers and party shoes. They gaze up at the coach with its posters and make one headlong rush for the doors like excited children, chattering and laughing. Lucky the driver isn't one of those grumpy types. People are still getting on, I had no idea so many people in Essex loved him. The shoppers are coming out now too with their array of baskets on wheels and plastic bags - all on the hunt for bargains.

Basildon's not a bad place to shop by any means. But for me the memories are mixed with ones of the mental health unit, of corridors and plastic seats and sweet machines; not too bad really. My other memories of the place have gone - lost somewhere with that part of me that was.

I wonder what it will be like. People have said in the chat room that he's just as amazing in person, if not more so. I hope I blend in; I don't want to stand out, not now. I feel like some broken down toy, not a member of this group.

I wonder how he feels. Is he nervous? I remember standing up on stage for a singing competition when I was a little girl. I was nervous at first, but with all the people down below and me away from them a little it felt all right after a while; it wasn't the same when my class were on the same level. If he's like me he must hate the Later with Jools Holland things.

How much we take for granted; a simple act like hopping on and off a bus or train can take ages now, and speaking on the phone for a taxi is non existent. When you're mentally disabled the mind sort of locks part of the time; you get what I call a 'white out' - no info just blank, like a blank cinema screen when they've all gone home. The main thing that gets me is that I can't travel far without someone with me, can't nip into shops or buy a ticket to somewhere, or drive - that's the partial sight kicking in too. It's like a cage and I'm not built for a cage!

The outlines of the buildings are becoming hazy now as the grey concrete bridge looms nearer, once under it we're really on our way. I can just see them setting up the market stalls as we turn down the road; the excitement's building again, if it ever stopped.

The houses lining the side of the road seem more rigid in their setting now, even trees look as though they were planted to order instead of growing naturally. There can't be too many people to go now as we're nearly full.

It's amazing when you think of it. There are coaches all around England just like ours, all filled with the same kind of people, all wanting the same the same kind of thing, if not on this night then on another near it. One person can do all that by a natural talent such as a voice, something we all use and very few have enough of to influence anyone, even if we tried.

A woman speaks up about how she would roam Basildon College dressed in silver space suits and red hair. She visited all the gigs she could, hitching rides to college to save money for them. We all laughed at the idea of her buying and wearing a black wig to go home in because her mother would have gone spare at the red. The wig matched her own hair colour and luckily her parents never noticed - not that she was at home that much, or when she was she was always in the bedroom fantasising.

"I drew a picture of him once." She said "Sent it to the fan club; probably thrown out by now or something. But it didn't stop me wanting him! He's so gorgeous!"

We stop for a few hours for food and stretching our legs; it's a good motorway café, fluorescent lights, metal and glass, and a tempting smell of fresh fruit and roast meat; we'll keep with our drinks and sandwiches, after all, there may be t-shirts or something and I'd rather use the food we've got than miss out on that. The toilets are white and clean with that sweet smelling pink soap on the wall in metal containers.

Shannon's browsing in a gift shop, all fluffy toys and porcelain; trust her to buy one of the Muppets! She laughs, walking Animal across the counter until the woman smiles and pushes it into a bag - its masses of hair having to be pushed in after it. She's mad and that's wonderful!

We're back on the coach now. It's dark and in the distance I can see the lights of the Birmingham NEC shining like a floodlit cathedral. Like Chaucer's pilgrims before me. I've arrived at my own personal Canterbury.

Life is a Lottery
by Doug Fraser

"I'm sorry, Mrs Williams," said Mr Cartwright, the store manager, in a nasal drone, "there isn't a nice way of saying it, so I'll come straight to the point. Your son has been caught stealing."

Jill felt her mouth go dry. "Is this true Sean?" she asked her teenage son sitting next to her.

"No it isn't!" hissed Sean. "I didn't steal!"

The manager's face took on a pained expression. He tapped a small package on the desk between them. "We have the evidence on film."

Jill could feel her hands shaking. The last four years had been difficult enough. First the discovery that Damon, her husband and Sean's father, was being unfaithful - with Tessa, her oldest friend, of all people. If that wasn't bad enough, finding her mother had known all along and chosen not to tell her of the affair, had been the final straw. Then the acrimonious divorce, and the struggle to keep the law practice going. And now this.

"How could you do this to me Sean?" she cried helplessly.

"I bought it Mum, he's lying!" protested Sean.

"Why would he lie?" she asked as calmly as she could.

Sean looked down at his boots and said nothing; his jaw clamped tight in teenage defiance. His behaviour had changed so much since the divorce that she couldn't believe he was the same loveable boy she'd adored from the moment the nurse placed him in her arms minutes after he was born. She could feel Damon's influence coming out in him.

"What exactly has he stolen?" she asked apprehensively.

"A lottery ticket." He held up a multi-coloured piece of paper. "And here is the Play Slip he left behind. That's how I knew the numbers he chose."

"A lottery ticket!" she laughed with the sheer relief of it. "You mean he bought a lottery ticket."

"Mum!" her son tugged her sleeve.

"Leave this to me, Sean," she pulled her sleeve clear, "I'm going to put this bumptious little man in his place!" She'd taken a dislike to the man the moment she'd met him. It wasn't just the nasal voice, or the white flabby hands he waved about as he spoke. It was more to do with the endless list of petty rules he'd expected her son to abide by before he'd allow him to deliver newspapers and for a pittance. The next few minutes were going to be a pleasure. She glared at Cartwright, "Do you mean to tell me you're going to take my child to court for one pound?" she spat the words at him. "It's hardly grand larceny, is it?"

Surprisingly, he didn't bat an eyelid.

She could feel the venom rising as she continued, "You know very well the law protects minors. It's your fault for selling it to him. I've a mind to take you to court myself!"

"Mum!" Sean's whisper increased to a shout. "It's the winning ticket!"

For a full five seconds the world stood still. She was aware of Sean's look of guilt and the store manager's look of malicious evil.

"Your son has illegally acquired a winning lottery ticket worth nine point three million pounds...." nasal voice intoned.

"But...but .." she squeaked lamely.

"He tried to threaten me Mum," whispered Sean, "to give him the ticket."

"Did you?" she turned to the manager.

"I was planning to inform you, after I'd confiscated the ticket. As evidence, of course."

"But you have no more right to it than Sean!"

"Now, now, now. Let's not be hasty. I shall use this evidence only if we cannot come to an arrangement," his voice oozed politeness. "Let me make a suggestion. You go up and claim the money Mrs Williams ... "

"It's my money!" protested Sean. "I won it!"

"But they won't pay you! You're too young!" growled nasal voice. "Now I suggest we share the winnings three ways - "

"No we won't!" screamed Sean.

"That way, we'll all benefit. You must make him see reason Mrs Williams...."

"How dare you make such a suggestion!" Jill was shocked by his words, "I'm a solicitor!"

"Mrs Williams, let us be practical. I'm sure you are the most moral and upright citizen. But the reality of the situation is that over nine million pounds is here, in this room, within our grasp." Jill thought carefully. The divorce settlement had seemed to favour her with a seventy-thirty split of the practice that she and Damon had built up from scratch. Only later had she realised that Damon's golfing and rugby friends were going to take all the corporate business away, leaving her to struggle by with a few conveyances and any passing trade. The future for her and Sean didn't look rosy. She knew she should go back and re-negotiate the divorce package, but pride stopped her.

"Of course, we could say nothing and do nothing. And the money will be given to charity in due course. All your son's cleverness in choosing the right numbers, will be given to someone else."

Cartwright was right. She examined the options. If she tried to collect the winnings on Sean's behalf, he'd report her and the scandal would ruin her. If she took him to court, he'd plead the child had used the lottery equipment when no one was watching. Once again, the money would go to charity.

And if she did nothing, would her son ever forgive her? In a year or two he'd want a flashy car and fine clothes to impress the girls with - well, the way the practice was going she couldn't see herself buying it for him. What if he turned to his father? She could feel her son being enticed away, leaving her with nothing to show for her life.

Yes, his proposal was illegal and went against all her instincts, her upbringing and training, but what choice did she have? This awful little man offered her the only way out of her dilemma. If she fell in with Cartwright's suggestions, Sean could have the future he deserved, and they could make a new life somewhere else. Somewhere where there was no extradition treaty with the U.K.

"Does anyone else know?" she asked.

"Would I be so careless?" he replied.

"How do I know I can trust you to keep quiet?"

"We have to trust each other Mrs Williams."

All Jill's instincts told her not to trust this man. Her upbringing; her professional training; her very moral fibre revolted against it...but...but ...the money would come in useful. She could take Sean away from the influence of his father. No more money worries. A life in the sun with the only human being she cared for - her son. But, could she pull it off?

Not so long ago, Jill would have said yes to that question. She remembered the times Sean deliberately chose to join her in the kitchen, making cakes, rather than join his father, in the lounge, watching football. The way he demanded a hug when the results were a success, which she readily gave. The pair of them revelling in the moment; she, at the surprising strength of his young body, bear-hugging her round the waist; he, glorying in her undivided love and attention.

But now he showed a starkly Victorian male attitude to life; that women should be grateful that some man had deigned to share their lives and should put up with any nasty things he got up to. That the divorce was her fault. Was this a passing phase in the passage from boyhood to manhood? Or was Damon's influence showing through?

"This shop has been a very lucky one for lottery winners," Cartwright's nasal drawl cut into her thoughts as though he'd been reading them. "We have had two Thunderball winners this year alone. And two second prizes in the main lottery last year. And countless smaller prizes, of course. So I know the set-up Mrs Williams. That's why I want a third of the prize money. I know how the Lottery people think. What questions they ask. What steps they take to verify the claim is genuine. You're paying for my expertise." He paused to let his words sink in. "Well? One third of the prize money to each of us in this room. Your son's share will be kept and used by you as you see fit. Do we have a deal?" He stood up and held a limp hand out to her. "Yes. Provided we have no publicity." Jill sighed with the relief of finally deciding. Somehow, in a perverse sort of way she knew she was going to enjoy being a rich criminal. She stood up and took his hand.

From the corner of her eye she saw Sean jump to his feet. "No deal! No deal! No deal!" he screamed, "It's my money and if I can't have it, no one can!"

He pulled the winning lottery ticket from his trouser pocket and tore it to shreds, scattering the pieces on the floor.

The Life and Soul of the Party

I've spent so much of my lifetime
Desperately wanting to be
The life and soul of the party
But sadly it wasn't me

I stand in the corner at parties
In the kitchen, by the sink
Wishing it soon to be over
And plying myself with drink

I've never been part of the in crowd
Never been part of the scene
I'm not your social animal
I'm not your party queen

It's taken a long time to get here
But finally I see
I don't need to be like everyone else
I'm okay being me

So to anybody out there
Who wants to be someone else
Stand up, be proud of who you are
It's great to be yourself

By Natalie Hudson

Sid the Sad Spook.
by G K Harris

Sid was a very unhappy ghost. He was unhappy because every time he tried to scare someone they just would not take him seriously.

He would appear in people's houses to try and scare them, but they would just look straight through him as if he wasn't there. He would hide down dark and eerie lanes, wait for someone to come along, then jump out on them.

"AHHH!" He would go in his most, scary voice. But that didn't work either. He even tried hanging around in churchyards, wailing and moaning. No self-respecting ghost would surely fail to scare someone in a churchyard, thought Sid. But, as usual, no one took the slightest bit of notice of him.

Sid sat on the churchyard wall feeling sorry for himself. He was just about to burst into tears when along came two children. They looked so scary. One was dressed as a werewolf, the other as a wicked witch. Sid took one look at them and screamed.

"EEK!" He went and fell off the graveyard wall.

"What was that, Micky?" the young girl asked her brother.

"Look, Abby, there's someone hiding behind the wall," he answered as he peered over the top.

"Hello. What's your name?" asked the boy. "Did we make you jump?" Sid popped his head up.

"My name's Sid, and yes you did," he said climbing back

onto the wall.

"Sorry, Sid," said the boy. "We didn't mean to scare you. You see we're only dressed up like you are for Halloween."

"Dressed up?" said Sid with a frown. "I don't know what you mean."

"You are pretending to be a ghost, aren't you?"

"What do you mean? Pretending to be a ghost," announced Sid loudly. "I am a ghost!" Gabby and Micky began to giggle.

"Why are you laughing at me?" Asked an even sadder Sid.

"Please don't be sad. We didn't mean to upset you. We only laughed because you're not scary enough to be a real ghost. You were more frightened of us than we were of you." This made poor Sid even more sadder.

"I know. That's why I'm so unhappy," said Sid. "I don't seem to be able to scare people." Micky winked at Gabby, then gave Sid a big friendly smile.

"It must be because you're too nice a ghost," he said, trying to cheer Sid up.

"Yeah, just because you're a ghost," said Gabby. "It doesn't mean that you have to go around scaring people."

"But ghosts are supposed to scare people," replied Sid with a sniffle, "but no one takes me seriously, all they do is laugh like you did."

"Well you are only little," said Gabby, "and to scare someone you really do have to want to. Do you really want to?" She asked.

"No, not really. I would much rather have fun, but how can a ghost have fun if he doesn't like scaring people?" Sid sighed. "Oh dear. I can't scare people, so I don't know how to have fun. What am I to do?" Poor old Sid looked like he was just about ready to burst into tears.

"Come on, Sid," said Gabby. "Please don't cry." Gabby and Micky felt sorry for Sid and decided they would play along with him. They still didn't think he was a real ghost, but a young boy who was all dressed up and didn't have any friends to celebrate Halloween with.

"Why don't you just pretend to be scary, like us?" Suggested Gabby. "We're going to have lots of fun, especially tonight."

"How?" asked Sid. "What's so special about tonight?" Micky and Gabby smiled at each other.

"Don't you know? Said Gabby. "Tonight is Halloween. The night we knock on doors and pretend to be scary."

"Yeah, and if we scare whoever opens the door enough," added Micky, " they give us a treat, or do a trick instead." Poor Sid was new at being a ghost. He didn't know about Halloween yet.

"That does sound like fun," he said. "But I don't have any friends to pretend with."

"Don't be silly Sid," said Gabby and Micky, "we're your friends now."

"WOW! Thank you. Thank you," said Sid very excitedly. He had never had friends before, especially two as nice as Gabby and Micky.

"Come on then Sid," said the children, as Sid jumped down from the wall. "Just do the same as we do." And off they went hopping and skipping down the street to the first house.

Knock, knock, knock. The door opened.

"Trick, or treat?" Shouted Gabby and Micky.

"Trick, or treat?" Copied Sid. The children laughed, because they were all supposed to shout it together. The nice lady didn't mind though. She pretended to be scared and was so impressed with their costumes, especially Sid's she smiled and gave them a big bar of chocolate each.

Sid was so excited. He had never had chocolate before. Once again they all danced and skipped down the street to the next house.

Knock, knock, knock. "Trick or treat?" This time they all shouted it together as a kindly looking man answered the door.

"Ah, yes, you're very scary," he said clapping his hands. Then he gave them a handful of toffees each.

"Thanks, mister," said Gabby and Micky. Sid couldn't say thanks though: He had all his toffees in his mouth at once and it was stuck, so he just tried to smile instead.

That night a happy Sid saw all sorts of monsters.

"They'er not usually friendly," he said, finally freeing his mouth. Gabby and Micky laughed.

"They're only pretend, remember?" Sid smiled.

"Come on race you," he shouted and this time was first to the door.

"Knock, knock, knock." But this time a rather bad tempered man answered, and before any of them had a chance to say a thing, the man began to shout at them.

"Sling yer 'ook," he bellowed and grabbed Micky by the ear. "Blooming 'orrible kids. Go an' pester someone else," he then yelled as he gave Micky's ear a nasty twist. Micky winced.

"Ouch! That hurt mister." The man was so horrible and terrified Gabby so much she started to cry.

This made Sid very angry. Gabby and Micky were his friends and he didn't like to see the nasty man upsetting, or hurting them. So, he disappeared just as the man tried to clip him round the ear too.

"Where'd he go?" Gasped the man. Sid quickly reappeared behind him and tapped him on the shoulder.

"BOO!" Went Sid, making the man jump. Then Sid made him float off the ground as he wailed and moaned in his best, ghostly voice. Then suddenly dropped him on his backside with a thump.

The man was no longer terrifying, but instead terrified as he ran inside his house and quickly slammed the door to get away from Sid. But it was no good because Sid stuck his head right through the door and blew a big, ghostly raspberry at him.

"Spluuurrr!" it went, the man ran upstairs to hide and this time he was so frightened by Sid' antics his face and his hair turned as white as Sid's.

Sid laughed. Gabby laughed and so did Micky.

"You really are a ghost," said Gabby.

"Yes, and you certainly put the wind up him," said Micky, "and he deserved it too. Thanks Sid."

"No," said Sid proudly. "I would like to thank you two, not only for being my friends and showing me how to have fun, but for giving me the opportunity to prove to myself that I can scare someone if I really want to, especially if they are as nasty as that man was.

"Please will you come and see us again Sid? Because we had fun too," asked the children.

"Of course I will," promised Sid. "I'll come and see you every Halloween. And if you ever need my help, all you have to do is shout this ghostly rhyme and I will always come and help you...

Sid the spook, Sid the spook, you are our friend so true.
We need you Sid, we need you Sid, please come and help us do."

Gabby and Micky waved at Sid as he disappeared into the night. And as he passed the full, bright moon he looked down and smiled broadly. Sid was now a very happy ghost.

The Homecoming
by Richard Banks

He never expected to return, neither had he wanted to, but someone had to pick up the pieces and as the beneficiary and executor of Julia's will he was the obvious and indeed the only candidate. She had, of course, intended to change her will and leave everything to her cousin Adele but the day to day complications of life after divorce had postponed longer term considerations to a day that had never arrived.

So here he was back at the house, key in hand, hoping that Julia hadn't changed the locks. There was, he thought, something different about the front door but when he inserted the key it opened stiffly and with its customary groan. There was a black stillness within and the smell of stale air. There were many demons in the house and he sensed them lurking in every dark corner. He reached out blindly for the light switch and caught it a glancing blow with the palm of his hand. The hall light flickered on and off, and then on again as his fingers made surer contact with the switch.

For a few moments he surveyed the familiar scene through which he had made anacrimonious exit some fifteen months earlier. The small, oval table which he had knocked over in his anger and frustration now supported a vase of withered carnations alongside the picture of a young man in his middle to late twenties. He looked briefly at the inscription on the photograph before placing it face down on the table. So this was Simon - Simon the racing driver, Simon the new love of Julia's life, devil-may-care Simon who had crashed his car extinguishing both his own life and that of Julia.

He had heard the news with an odd confusion of emotions. He had felt sadness. Yes he definitely felt sadness, but he also felt anger and hatred. Hatred for Simon, hatred for Julia and an absence of self esteem that bordered on revulsion. In time it would all make sense but that time was not now. His memories were too fresh, too painful. What had happened had happened, he told himself. Don't analyse it, what's the point, there's no going back.

He moved on into the lounge. There was a new picture above the fireplace and an empty space where his computer had once stood - the computer that he had bought without consulting Julia, the computer which she had resented almost as much as she later resented him. Its arrival had signalled the end of the beginning. Thereafter they were two separate people with diverging interests struggling to co-exist in the same space. He poured himself a drink from the half empty bottle of Jack Daniels that he had found in the wall unit and sipped it slowly, subconsciously putting off the moment when he would go upstairs. Upstairs memories were the worse, the memories of what might have been.

He hoped it would be different now but as he mounted the stairs he sensed that nothing had changed. He immediately went to the smaller of the two bedrooms and found himself staring at the same tragic scene - the Winnie the Pooh wallpaper and curtains, the large mobile above the cot and the brightly painted cupboard full of toys and baby clothes. His mind went back to that cold January day when, late in her pregnancy, Julia had miscarried baby Thomas. It was a tragedy from which she was never to fully recover. He should have been kinder, more understanding - he realised that now - but she had made it so difficult for him: her black moods, her emotional outbursts, her unconcealed coldness towards him. Six months later, when he could bear it no longer, he had packed a suitcase and stormed angrily out of the house.

He resisted the urge to punch the wall and instead crossed the landing to the other bedroom, the inner sanctum he had shared with Julia. He pushed the door open and peered inside at the unmade bed, the carelessly discarded clothing and the curtains billowing gently in front of the open windows. He pictured the sequence of events that had claimed the lives of Julia and Simon. They had only meant to stay an hour but had lingered too long, half asleep in each others arms and then one of them had woken, glanced disbelievingly at the bedside clock and hurriedly roused the other. They were late, late in starting out for that special concert that Julia so wanted to see. Abandoning the crumpled sheets they rapidly dressed, several minutes of frantic activity before neighbours saw them burst out of the house and speed off in Simon's Ferrari. Other witnesses saw them end their journey on the A127 near North Benfleet. Simon had been driving too fast, recklessly fast according to the Police. There had been a car in the outside lane that wouldn't let Simon through. Instead of slowing down he had attempted to pass it on the inside careering into another vehicle and ricocheting, with devastating impact, into the side of a bridge.

He felt a strange compulsion to remake the bed as if that would somehow erase the memory of what had happened but that was not the reason why he had come. There were papers in the bedside cabinet that he needed to retrieve before others found them; papers which related to his previous employment with Fenton Motors. He had not been there when Simon brought in his car for servicing; in fact he had not set foot in the place for over a year. He had just started a job in Colchester when the agency told him to drop everything and get over to Fenton's who urgently needed an experienced mechanic. At first, the name on the worksheet had meant nothing to him, then someone mentioned that the car belonged to a Formula 3 racing driver.

That was all he needed to make the connection; it was that Simon, the Simon who had finally wrecked any chance of a reconciliation with Julia.

In the middle of an otherwise faultless service he partially sheared through one of the brake cables ensuring its eventual failure. He hadn't meant to kill Julia. That had never been part of his plan but now that it had happened he felt strangely free of guilt. He wondered how this could be.

Then he understood. It was meant to be. It was fate, not chance, that had entrusted him with the maintenance of Simon's car. It was fate that had concealed all evidence of his lethal surgery within the mangled wreckage. Fate had vindicated him, had shown him the way and was now providing closure. "It's over," he heard himself murmur. At long last it was over.

He closed the bedroom windows and retraced his steps through the house, turning off the lights as he did so. Tomorrow he would arrange for the house to be cleared. That done, he would put it up for sale. There was much to do and for the moment doing was better than thinking.

> A young politician called Blair,
> once fell fast asleep in a chair.
> Said Cherie in a tizzy,
> "wake up and get busy,
> You won't get elected from there."
> Peter Freeman.

The Old Sycamore Tree

Sometimes I think of the old tree again,
Stretching its branches in the wind and the rain.
Through winter days when covered with snow,
Trying to protect all that nested below.

From the dark days of war, to the Victory cheers,
It still stood defiant through my childhood years.
In the grey-backed houses where we lived out our lives,
It showed us the seasons and how to survive.

With the factory's smoke that invaded each day,
The Victorian houses began to decay.
We all had to move from the friends we had known,
The community gone, the tree stood alone.

by Sis Unsworth

Traffic
by Richard Banks

In the distance he could hear traffic; a dull, hissing fusion of sound - the drone of engines, the displacement of air on a shrill winter's morning, the sound of rubber tyres over wet tarmac. All largely unheard, save for the occasional wail of sirens and the squeal of sudden braking.

Hotel Paradiso
by Bernice Bedford

"Hallo, Ms Julius? It's Emma Fox here, giving you an update. Yes, yes, still hot on his trail. At the moment, I'm sitting in the foyer of a horribly run-down little establishment on the Kent coast, near Margate. Your husband's just checked in and gone up to his room. Yes, he has some luggage, just a couple of cases that's all. What do you mean, bug the room? I'm a one-woman band private eye, not MI5. Okay, I'll do my best. Bye."

Folding shut her mobile, Emma sighed. Why do I never attract high profile sex scandals with Tory MPs or big drugs scams with the rich and famous? My work is one round of routinely unfaithful partners and missing mongrels. And this looks like being another much the same.

She glanced around the shabby little reception area of the 'Hotel Paradiso'. Someone has a sense of humour, she thought. The décor's more suited to a fifties sit-com, with a receptionist to match. Sort of Bates Motel meets Terry and June. Let's hope my room is more appealing.

Damn Ms Julius and her wandering toy-boy, she reflected, entering the surprisingly neat hotel bedroom. Better known as Janey Julius, sometime star of stage, screen and musical, Janey had met Sam during a run of her one woman show, hopefully entitled: 'Andy and Janey - a tribute to Andrew Lloyd Webber and his Music.' Sam was one of the lighting crew, young, tall, fit and available. Emma could fancy him herself in different circumstances.

Janey's first husband had also been her agent and died very suddenly, leaving her a great deal of money but a rapidly fading career. Sam provided the attention she so desperately needed. Friends said he appeared to adore her - although no longer young, she was still a very attractive woman, with an even more attractive bank balance.

The receptionist, a vision in tangerine, managed to tear herself away from reading a well-thumbed copy of 'The Naked Ape,' and smiling brightly, handed over the keys. As she did so, Emma was able to catch a glance at the register and, memorising Sam's room number, strode off to her room to write up her findings.

After dinner, Emma lay on the surprisingly comfortable bed, kicking off her shoes and pondering her next move. She had tried to catch Sam's eye during the evening meal but to no avail. He just devoured all three unimaginative courses, hardly looking up, and after a quick cup of coffee left the restaurant making for the stairs. Alone.

She bought a drink and lingered at the bar in order to see if he returned from his room or left the hotel. He didn't. And no young girl arrived looking for a clandestine night of passion, either. Seemed like another dead end. The bar was filling up but not with any suitable candidates. Mostly men, and they looked like a convention of organic butchers on an overnighter. Where to go from here?

She was not going to try the 'morning tea routine' again. Not after that last time in Morecombe Bay. Having managed, with great difficulty, to get hold of a uniform and a tray of tea by seven in the morning, she had knocked on the door of her quarry.

Hearing nothing after many knocks, she burst in dramatically only to find his naked dead body lying on the bed before her, eyes staring glassily at the ceiling. Highly embarrassing. Apparently, not feeling well while travelling home from a conference, he had booked into the nearest hotel. During the night he suffered a major heart attack. Well, he might have locked his door first, Emma mused. Worst of all, she had felt too mortified to demand payment from the widow.

No, it had to be the old 'wrong room' trick, she thought. I'll go down around midnight, looking a little the worse for drink and knock on his door. " Oh sorry", I'll say, "How stupid of me. You must forgive me - my friend is staying here and I seem to have the room numbers mixed up. Too long in the bar I'm afraid". That would give me long enough for a good look round for any signs of a female presence or play away accessories.

Full of optimism, Emma left her room, hair in disarray and clever usage of rouge perfectly creating a three sheets to the wind appearance. Room one twenty one, here I come, she muttered cheerfully to herself in the lift.

"Okay. Okay, Ms Julius. I'm sorry, I know it's a terrible shock. Of course, I had no idea. At least you know where he goes now and why. Well, try to look on the positive side. He isn't being unfaithful and he loves you very much. And it's good for men to have a hobby. Well, maybe it's not one you would choose, but he has promised to return all your clothes. And the wigs borrowed from the wardrobe department. No harm done then. Well, yes, of course. It throws rather a different light on your relationship. But some men are made that way. Quite a lot judging by the number in Sam's room last night. Sorry, sorry. I didn't mean to be flippant. They were hard to recognize under all that make-up, but I think I can safely say they were the same guys I saw in reception earlier. I did wonder why a male overnighter needed quite so many shopping bags. Yes, Ms Julius. Sorry Ms Julius. Now, about my remittance."

Purr-fect Pet

I'm creeping silently through the house,
Searching for prey; a bug, a mouse.
I end up perched upon the shelf,
And care for no-one but myself.

I lick my paw and clean my fur,
I make no sound but my incessant purr.
I sniff the air around the house,
Searching, searching for that mouse.

My boredom shows, a nap I think!
My fluffy self grabs forty winks.
I find a pillow, the softest type,
And dream up visions of rodent hype.

Maybe later I'll hunt again,
But not outside, not in the rain.
Instead I'll sleep the day away,
And search tomorrow for my prey.

by S J Banham

VILLEGGIATURA IN VALDINIEVOLE
© 2004 Charles L. Joseph

Think of Tuscany and immediate thoughts of Florence spring to mind. Described as a living canvas and, of course, known as the birthplace of the Renaissance, you could be forgiven for being drawn to this sophisticated, world-renowned city. A city, which, with her grand palaces, churches and priceless art collections, cannot fail to impress.

I too enjoyed the views and sounds of Florence during my assignment there, but when searching for a place to live, I really wanted the luxury of being within easy commuting distance from my office and yet be somewhere strategically well placed to reach other parts of Tuscany.

VALLEY OF MISTS

Montecatini Terme is set against the backdrop of picturesque hills in the Valdinievole (Valley of Mists), some forty Kilometres west of Florence. I first discovered this elegant and leafy spa resort in the summer of 1998 and was immediately impressed by its elegance and by how green and well manicured the public park and gardens were. Although relatively modern by Tuscan standards, the town has a fascinating historical and cultural background. I made my choice.

Here, I could enjoy town life intermingled with country life and so decided to make Montecatini my base for the duration.

CHANGING FORTUNES

Reputed to be a popular spa during Roman times, the town declined. During the Middle Ages much of the area was covered by marshland. This brought about the inevitable onslaught of malaria and decay. Although some minor improvements were ordered by Cosimo de' Medici during the sixteenth century, most of the area's development is really owed to the intervention of Grand Duke Pietro Leopoldo I who, by initiating a new wave of renovation and construction in 1772, provided much firmer foundations than that of earlier years.

Nothing was to be quite the same for Montecatini. In a gradual upsurge of popularity it was to become in its heyday, a fashionable resort for the rich and famous. Devotees of the good life; here they would come to take the waters with curative powers (the minerals apparently promise relief from stomach and liver disorders) and also to indulge in other leisurely activities. Famous personalities that have been associated with Montecatini Terme include Giuseppe Verdi who came here regularly throughout the last eighteen years of his life.

PLENTY OF CHOICE

There would be little point in visiting Montecatini Terme without sampling the spring waters or rejuvenating your mind, body and soul in one of the many therapeutic centres on offer. Now one of Italy's largest spa resorts, it is also strategically well placed to reach Pisa, Lucca and Florence by road or by rail. The centre of town is a "shopofile's" paradise; the fine boutiques scattered along the main streets of Corso Matteotti and Corso Roma are like powerful magnets enticing you to be tempted by a broad range of beautiful things. This is a place where you can literally shop until you drop, so don't leave home without your credit cards!

The scores of bars and cafés here are stuffed with tempting and delicious things to eat (the best known are the cialde, sweet, wafer-like biscuits) but perhaps the most celebrated of them all is the Café Pasticceria Giovannini, whose cakes are absolutely exquisite and the best I've tasted. Graziano Giovannini has also won numerous awards for his famous sculptures. Using chocolate and icing sugar he has constructed many of Italy's famous buildings, the most spectacular of these sculptures being Pisa's Piazza dei Miracoli.

Montecatini presents the visitor with a tantalising choice of hotels, restaurants, osterias and trattorias. They are everywhere and you can't avoid them. I have my personal favourites: the Grand Hotel Vittoria for its classical charm and the Grand Hotel Ambasciatori (the tallest building in town) for its splendid rooftop views. For genuine Tuscan cuisine as well as ambience, I prefer Ristorante Pietre Cavate or Ristorante Montacolle, both offering magnificent views of the Valdinievole.

GARDENS AND PALACES

There are nine spa establishments in Montecatini and two in nearby Monsummano Terme. Beautifully set amongst colourful gardens, studded with rich and fascinating buildings, the Stabilimento Tettuccio with its monumental façade adorned with intricate sculptures, pilasters and windows is for me the most grandiose looking of all. Its origins date back to the sixteenth century, although it was later modified during the early part of the twentieth. During the spring and summer months, pretty floral displays decorate Viale Verdi, and the lush oasis of the Parco Termale offers a much-needed respite under the cool shade of the leafy canopy of trees.

If you fancy a foray into the past then standing vigil 300 metres above town is the medieval village of Montecatini Alto. From the vantage point of Via Vittorio Veneto you get uninterrupted and spectacular views across the valley, but what remains clear in my mind is the village lit up at night with its unusual spiral of streetlights, almost as if it were a UFO. Once almost totally destroyed as a result of the battles that waged between Guelphs and Ghibellines, the entire hamlet now represents an interesting fusion of ancient and modern buildings. As you dip into the intricate, narrow streets you will discover fascinating gems like the remains of an ancient castle, the Torre dei Lemmi, the church of San Pietro, and the Teatro dei Risorti in Piazza Giusti.

LET THE TRAIN TAKE THE STRAIN

For me, the most enjoyable way to get to the top is to take the ten-minute trip on the funicular railway from the lower station in Viale Diaz (open April to October only). Inaugurated in 1898 the railway has truly stood the test of time. On a hot summer evening, a ride to the summit inside one of these bright red cars, either "Gigio" or "Gigia", is a treat not to be missed. Those of you feeling energetic enough can also trek up to the top via the steep path through the olive groves running alongside the funicular. It is an invigorating walk. And if you are still sufficiently fit, I recommend the return route down Via Maona.

WARRIORS AND POETS

Continue east and you will reach the hilltop village of Serravalle Pistoiese. Yet another pawn in the constant struggle for supremacy between Pisa, Lucca and Florence, the village extends across from the gentler northern slopes of Monte Albano and is typical of the many defensive hilltop sites that are scattered throughout Tuscany. Here, the remains of two strategic fortifications - the Rocca Vecchia and the Rocca Nuova - that once encircled the entire village are still visible. Serravalle literally means, "locked valley": an appropriate name since the two fortresses played a major role in controlling the main east-west communications route by blocking the entire valley. They comprised the central stronghold and defensive system for the whole area.

The smaller spa town of Monsummano Terme lies to the south. It was originally an eleventh century fortress situated on top of a hill dominating the Padule di Fucecchio and the Valdinievole. Named after the Castello di Montessomano, which for a short period belonged to the Abbey of Sant' Antimo in the Val d'Orcia, it was sold to Lucca in 1218. Because of its strategic position, it also aroused great interest from Florence. In an attempt to keep the Florentines out Monsummano later joined the league of Valdinievole.

In the fifteenth century a rural town, today it is a deceptively busy place. The main attractions for the visitor being the limestone caves, to be found in the immediate area, which now provide the thermal grotto's known as "Paradiso", "Purgatorio" and "Inferno" (so called to commemorate Dante and his Divine Comedy).

FUN, FOOD AND GOOD FRIENDS

Living in Montecatini has definitely left its mark and I have acquired a deep affection for the area. If my villeggiatura in Valdinievole could be compressed into a single experience, it would have to be the many pleasurable hours spent over an excellent lunch or dinner with my friends in Monsummano. I certainly miss the wonderful risottos and other interesting dishes that my friend Marcella used to prepare!

Greed

It possesses you
Controls you
Engulfs you

Gives you strength
Passion
Purpose

Fills you with fear
Dread
Anxiety

Makes you feel helpless
Empty
Broken

Leaves you selfish
Miserable
Alone

By Natalie Hudson

By The Sea Shore
by Gwenda Syratt

She sat in a brown and orange striped deckchair with her bare legs raised by resting them on the sea wall, drifting between private thoughts and reading her book, she felt very content.

"What a beautiful day" she said to herself and felt a thrill in her heart as she watched the sun rays dancing on the waves, giving the illusion that sparkling diamonds live in the sea. There was a gentle on shore breeze, just enough to keep unwanted insects at bay, a truly perfect day.

She watched sparrows searching for food on the promenade and took a biscuit from her lunch box, after crushing it into a thousand pieces, she scattered it on the ground. The sparrows were brave and came close to her deckchair until the larger starlings took their place. Seagulls dipped and dived above her head but lacked the courage to land on the pavement. She would save some bread from her lunch and place it on the sea wall for them later.

"Oh what bliss!" she thought, so peaceful this time of the year with children safely cocooned at school and adults demanding an audience for their conversation at an alternative location.

"Excuse me" a deep voice called from somewhere behind her head. She jumped up and saw a man wearing a straw trilby hat, shorts and cotton shirt straddled across the apex of a beach hut with no means of getting down. "I feel rather foolish, my ladder has fallen and it's one hell of a jump! Would you mind?"

She ran to his aid and picked the heavy ladder up and placed it firmly at the side of the beach hut enabling the man to place an uncertain foot onto the top rung.

"You're a star!" he said, "I could have been up there for hours!"

"Not really", she said giving a more accurate report, "Someone walking a dog would soon come along and rescue you."

"Mmmm", he snorted, "It was a dog that pushed the ladder away, I'm glad you were here to save me."

She felt slightly uneasy, she hated anything close to a personal remark and so she just smiled and began to walk back to her chair.

"I wonder if you could just spare a couple of minutes," he said. "I'm trying to get this sheeting to cover the roof but the breeze is making it difficult single handed."

"What would you like me to do?" she asked. "I'm hopeless at D.I.Y."

"If you could just steady that corner of the sheeting it would make all the difference."

They worked together for twenty minutes, neither speaking as both were concentrating on the task.

At last he said, "There! Last tack, a lovely smooth job, we deserve a coffee break don't you think?"

He wasn't really asking her opinion, but telling her he was making coffee and disappeared inside the wooden hut. She could hear the pop of the calor gas stove and the chink of the china and within minutes of returning to her deckchair, she heard the kettle whistle.

He came towards her carrying a tray with coffee and biscuits and placed it on the sea wall. Then he returned to the hut and, after bringing out another chair, settled comfortably beside her.

"Thanks for your help", he said, "You really have saved me a lot of time."

"I enjoyed it", she said and meant it.

"Are you retired?" He asked, "And enjoying your freedom?"

"Yes and yes!" she replied and suddenly she began to tell him how afraid she had been of ending her working life, how desperate and worthless she had felt when leaving the school after a life-time of teaching. how she had been completely ignorant of leisurely pleasures and the luxurious feeling of wasting time.

"Yes" he agreed softly, "there is a lot more to life than working for money."

"Oh I had job satisfaction," she replied hastily, "It is just that it has taken me thirty five years to realise that my world was so narrow and, well, responsible."

"Well" he said with a smile, "most of us take thirtyfive years to wake up to some facts of life, better late than never they say." They chatted on amicably about their lives and inner most thoughts completely out of character for these two souls to be in harness so soon. She didn't have to ask, he was open and direct. "My wife died three years ago after a very long fight against cancer."

He quickly changed the tempo of the conversation. "She loved it here at the beach hut. The sea, the birds, the peace and the sunshine. Always something to see and do and company to enjoy. "That's why we called our hut "Happy Talk."

She glanced over to the beach hut and the name was written in a South Sea Pacific island style.

"I've never married" she said, and immediately wondered

why she had been so outspoken. She often felt embarrassed about being unmarried but didn't know why, even though she had analysed the situation from every aspect from time to time.

He spoke about his difficulty in learning to live alone after a lifetime with one woman, how he longed to share the most simple pleasures of life. He said his sister had been very good at keeping him involved with family life and suddenly jumped up from the chair and onto his feet.

"Speak of the Devil!" he exclaimed, "There IS my sister!"

A tall slim woman approached wearing navy trousers and a red and white cotton top. Her skin was very tanned for this time of year indicating many hours spent in the open air. She had a lovely smile and looked quizzically at them both. After the introductions, a third chair was placed by the sea wall and happy talk continued to flow between them.

The sun moved from east to west in the sky and reached its highest point. An umbrella on a stand was brought to the sea wall to protect the three from the strong sun rays.

"Did I see you with a lunch box?" He asked, "May we share? We have plenty of tea, coffee, milk cheese and biscuits but no bread".

"Of course!" She said, "Let's share".

After lunch she kept her promise to the seagulls, and they squawked and screeched with pleasure and appreciation.

They strolled along the promenade whilst the sister washed the dishes and returned to the hut walking along the waters edge. As the sun began its descent in the sky, it was time for afternoon tea and the sea had retreated leaving mud and sea weed along the shore line.

Still talking happily, the ebbing tide moved further into the distance leaving sailing and fishing boats resting awkwardly on the mud. Dark silhouettes of people could be seen raking cockles or just walking to feel the soft squelchy mud between their toes.

"Goodness" she said looking at her wrist watch and jumping to her feet. "I've been here ALL day."

"Yes, and hasn't it been lovely," he said. "Please come and see us again, we have enjoyed your company."

"Thank you," she said and lifted her chair and lunch box to take them to her car. She said nothing, but she knew she would see him again.

Whilst the sister packed the chairs away in the beach hut, he bent down to the cupboard that housed the Calor gas canister to turn the tap to off.

He looked up and smiled at her. "Thanks Sis."
"Woof, Woof !" she barked. "I'm glad that moving the ladder worked!"

Abandoned

Mandy looked across the room at them, feeling incredibly guilty. They were her friends - they had seen her through many bad times in her life, comforted her, and now she was planning to turn her back on them for good. But she had no choice - she was slimming, and there was no room in her life any more for biscuits.

by Amanda Gooden

The Unattainable

I have a good life
Lovely wife, two kids
Roof over my head
And a fancy car
But I want more

I want a Caribbean holiday
Convertible sports car with personalised plates
Place in the country with maids and a gardener
Model wife who all my friends envy me for being with
Perfect kids who don't show me up in public

I have a good job
Friendly colleagues
A fair boss
Nice location
Average pay
But I want more

I want a company car that's better than the boss's
My own office with my name on the door
All my colleagues to call me 'Sir' and hold doors open for me
To work extra short days near the beach on a tropical island
My wages to be doubled with a huge monthly bonus added

I want, I want, I want
It's all just greed
Funny thing is, if I had it all I'd just want more
I think I'll stick with what I've got

By Natalie Hudson

George and the Giant
by Bob French

George frantically wrapped his aching arms around his knees and pulled them up tight to his chest trying to push himself further back into the corner of the dark, damp, dirty coal scullery. In desperation he tried to control the thumping of his heart and his erratic breathing, but failed. He could hear the rattle of doors and vile threats as the gang approached his hiding place. Suddenly the old wooden door rattled violently, spraying dust into the cold dank atmosphere of his hiding place.

"Come on Frampton. We know you're here!" George closed his eyes, buried his face into his dirty knees and prayed. The world stood still for a brief second, then the sound of his pursuers started to fade and he slowly let out a deep breath, allowing his head gently to loll back and rest against the coal stained wall. The threat had passed.

George Frampton waited another half an hour before plucking up enough courage to struggle to his feet and cautiously open the door of the scullery. Though the brightness of the afternoon sun briefly took his sight, his ears were straining for sounds of danger. A quick glance both ways told him it was safe to make his escape and, with the speed of an Olympic athlete, George sprinted for home.

"Have you been playing rugby with James and his friends

again?" His Mother's eyes rolled as she looked at his dirt covered pullover and shorts. "I've told you before. You're not to play in your school clothes. Now go out the back and give yourself a scrub. Supper will be ready in a minute."

After helping his mother to wash up the dishes, George threw an extra log in the kitchen stove then made him self comfortable at the large oak kitchen table and read for the umpteenth time his album 'The Wheatherstone Falcons Rugby League Football Club.' It had been a present from his father. George was proud of the fact that his father had taken him to every home game since he was five, but after his death in a mining accident last year, there had been very few luxuries. George helped out by doing a morning paper round and a Saturday job delivering for old Mr Jenkins, the butcher. He heard his mother's tired footsteps as they started to climb the creaky stairs.

"Don't be late, George. You've got school tomorrow."

"I won't be, Mum." But George had a problem that had been bothering him for a while. For the first time in the club's history the Falcons had made it through to the semi finals of the Champion's Cup. He desperately wanted to go but hadn't enough money to buy a ticket. George decided to ask Mr Jenkins if he could have his next two Saturday's wages in advance. Confident that he had solved his problem, he quietly closed the well-thumbed book, turned down the lamp and followed his mother upstairs.

George smiled to himself on the way home. He had had a good day at school; avoided the bullies, received a good mark for his arithmetic and to crown it all he managed secretly to meet Heather. They had know each other since junior school and their friendship had grown to something a little more than best friends. But, much to Heather's protests, George still insisted that they should not be seen together at school for fear of the bullies. Such days warranted a reward he though to himself as he turned into the corner shop. The tin bell announced his entrance just as an old lady, who was struggling with her groceries, dropped everything. The brown paper bag split on impact, sending the potatoes and brussels sprouts dancing in all directions across the shop floor and the few coins she had scattered everywhere. Without thinking George lent down and helped pick up the groceries and her money.

"That'll be two shillings and six pence halfpenny please love." The old lady fumbled for a while then started to look down at the floor.

"Oh dear, I seem to be missing sixpence." Without thinking, George put his hand in his pocket, took out his sixpenny piece and gave it to her. The old lady stared at him, then lent forward and thanked him quietly. George realising that he hadn't the money to treat himself anymore and decided to get on home, avoiding the Butler Estate, where he knew the bullies roamed.

The rain had started to ease just as George pushed the old delivery bike into the back yard behind the butcher's shop.

"Well done George." Old Mr Jenkins wiped his hands on his now blood-stained white apron and fumbled in his pocket. "Two weeks wages as agreed lad." With a jingling of coins he handed him five shillings. "I suppose you've got enough for a ticket to the semi finals now?" George didn't have to say anything. The smile on his face told Old Mr Jenkins everything. George pocketed the silver coins and quickly glanced at the shop clock. The butcher, reading the boys thoughts, sighed.

"Ay lad, if you're quick enough you might catch the ticket office before it closes."

"Thanks Mr Jenkins. You're a sport." With that, George tore off his apron, threw his wet cap into the basket of the black butcher's bike and sprinted for the back gate. It wasn't until he turned the corner and saw the flags of the rugby ground in the distance that he realised he was on the outskirts of Butler Estate. Before George could retrace his steps, a grubby hand gripped his shoulder and forced him up against the wall, a ringing slap caught George across his face bringing tears to his eyes. He looked up into the face of one of the Milligan brothers; part of the gang of bullies who tormented him at school.

"What are you doing in our part of town Frampton? We told you that if you ever came over here, you'd be for it."

Other boys started to gather around him and someone pushed him violently. His head cracked against the wall and he slid to the ground. George hit the hard pavement slab and saw stars, then felt a sharp pain as someone kicked him in the chest. He clenched his eyes shut and gasped for breath as he felt rough hands going through his pockets. He heard their laughter and hoots of joy as they realised their luck. In the distance George heard people yelling at the attackers and felt them push away from him, yelling abuse and foul language as they ran off across the heath. He seemed to lie there for a while, then opened his eyes and stared up at the clear blue sky. Strangers had started to gather. George attempted to get up, but all that did was to bring a stinging pain to his chest, and he let out a low scream, closed his eyes and lay back down again. He heard someone say they should call a doctor. Then through the distant sounds of the concerned crowd he heard Heather's voice." George. George are you all right dear?" He opened his eyes and looked into her face. She smiled down at him and brushed the hair from his eyes.

"You all right?" He could hear the concern in her voice as she slid her hand under his head.

"They've stolen all my money." She eased him up slowly into the sitting position.

"Heather. They've stolen my money."

"It doesn't matter about the money. As long as you're all right." He groaned as he struggled to get to his feet and winced at the throbbing pain in his chest.

"They've stolen my money. The money I needed for the semi final ticket. It's all gone."

"It doesn't matter any more George, the only thing that matters is getting you home. Come on." Heather put her arm around his shoulders and gently guided him across the road.

"Come on. I don't live far." It suddenly occurred to George that he didn't actually know where Heather lived. He thought they must have walked half a mile, but in fact they had walked about fifty yards to the door of Heather's home. She struggled with George as she climbed the two steps that lead to the front door of her home and pushed it open. They fell into the front passage. It was dark and the house smelt of freshly baked cakes. Suddenly a door at the far end of the passage opened throwing light on them. There, standing in the doorway of the kitchen was the old lady who had dropped her groceries in the corner shop.

"Hello pet, what's this then?" Heather gasped out as she struggled to her feet.

"Sorry, Nanna. George had a bit of a run in with the Milligan brothers. Beat him up and took his money."

"I'm all right, really I am." George tried to straighten up, but felt light headed and slumped down between the two of them. When he finally regained his senses he was sitting on the settee in front of a raging fire in the front room.

"I know you." The old lady lent forward to take a closer look at him. "You're the lad who helped me out at the shop." The old lady turned to Heather. "Remember, pet, I told you about this nice young lad. He gave me sixpence." Heather tilted her head, looked down at the boy she had become very fond of and smiled.

"Right little knight in shinning armour, aren't you George."

Once he had rested and downed two glasses of sweet soda water, Heather took George out into the back garden and they sat on the garden bench under the shade of the tall apple tree. They talked for hours about anything and nothing. George had never enjoyed himself so much. He suddenly noticed that the shadow of the fence had engulfed the whole garden telling him that it was time to make his way home.

"I'll walk you home." George started to protest but then looked up into her face and realised that it was not a request and nodded.

Just as they were leaving the old lady asked George if he would like to come to tea next Saturday. George was about to say that he was going to the semi finals, then realised that he didn't have the money anymore to buy the ticket.

"Yes, I'd love to come."

"Fine then. I will see you at two o'clock then and thank you for helping me last week. I really do appreciate it young man."

Saturday afternoon could not come quickly enough. As George carefully made his way through the back streets to Heather's home, he felt saddened as he came up on fathers and their sons making their way towards the rugby ground, wishing his father were here to take him, yet he also felt happy at the prospect of spending some time with Heather.

At exactly two o'clock, George knocked on Heather's front door. As he stepped into the darkened passageway, she lent forward and quickly kissed him on the cheek. He had never been kissed before, well, not by a girl. Heather grabbed his hand and guided him into the front room where Heather's grandma was sitting having a cup of tea.

"Hello George, come in. Sit your self down. Scone?" She nodded toward the freshly baked pile of scones that sat pyramid-like on her best china plate. The sound of the front door opening caused Heather to jump up from her chair. The door to the front room opened and a giant of a man stooped to enter the room. The deep voice boomed out.

"Hi Nan. You all right?" The expression on the old lady's face was one of joy as she stood up and greeted her grandson. She waited until be bent down and allowed her to reach up and kiss his cheek. George was dumbstruck.

"George, this is my grandson, Michael Collins." They said his surname together.

"Tight head prop, joined the Falcons from Bradford in '34. Twenty eight tries." George rattled off the statistics as though he were a computer.. The tall man laughed.

"Good to see you're up on the game, George," and extended his massive hand. George took it, but had to pinch himself afterwards just to make sure he wasn't imagining things.

"Now come on, you haven't got much time." The old lady fussed as she looked at George and Heather. "Kick Off is in an hour's time, so you mustn't be late."

George looked up in confusion, then realised what the old lady had just said. Then in his excitement dropped his plate of scones onto the carpet.

"Yes, George. Michael and Heather are taking you to the semi finals." George looked at Heather then at the smiling giant. He still couldn't believe his ears. Then, as if by some secret signal, they all burst into laughter.

They parked on the edge of the car park so as to avoid the crowds and walked the last hundred yards to the VIP entrance of the Falcons rugby ground. Just as they approached the queues of spectators, George spotted the bullies who had beaten him up and stolen his money and waited until they had seen him. Then turning to Michael who took one step to four of theirs:

"Michael, do you think you could say hello to some of my

friends," and purposefully pointed towards the group of bullies. The tall hard-faced man nodded and changed direction and started to walk directly towards the group of bullies. Their chanting and yelling fell silent as they realised that George and this giant of a man were now walking directly towards them. Fearing revenge was about to be taken out on them they fled in terror.

The Falcons won their game, and George and Heather enjoyed the afternoon. On Monday George met Heather at the corner of the school fence and they walked hand in hand up to the main gate. The Milligan brothers and their hangers-on were there as usual, only this time they parted to allow them through. Tug Milligan, the eldest brother looked up from nervously studying the ground and in a less than confident voice asked if he was all right. George looked him in the eye and smiled, squeezing Heather's hand gently.

"Fine thanks." George stole a glance at Heather. Life was going to be much better around here he thought.

Murder

Peter felt nothing as he pulled the trigger and watched John's lifeless body fall to the floor. Stella's face was a picture, believing that she was next. It wasn't the first time he had done this, and it wouldn't be the last. There was one performance each night, and a matinee on Wednesday. He had Sunday's off.

by Amanda Gooden

Getting Published
by Bernice Bedford

It lies on the tiled floor like a dead fish waiting to be gutted, a white oblong with small italic printing. I look down and recoil. It isn't a bill so it is probably a rejection. Another wretched rejection. I ought to be used to this by now. A few generous people encouraging me in a writing group doesn't mean the whole world will be fascinated by my pathetic ramblings.

Eventually, I pick up the envelope and tear irritably at the ribbed paper. Through half closed eyes I read the contents. Surely not. I read it through again, eyes wide open now. My God, they're interested. In me, my writing, my story.

Telephone in hand, I try to punch the number with shaking fingers. What's the betting I've misunderstood - haven't read the small print or something.

"Hello, this is Luke Westwood. Yes, that's right. What? Yes. Yes, of course. I'll be there. Four o'clock Friday." Amazing.

It appears a small publisher of new crime really likes my work and is very interested in the manuscript I sent him. I am going to meet the editor this week. This is a life changing moment and deserves a real celebration - I'll see if there's any red wine left and finish up the rest of that Kit Kat. Someone up there loves me. Yes!

That "someone" turns out to be an untidy sandy-haired little man with side whiskers and a limp. He offsets this by using a wonderfully ornate silver walking stick, almost as antique as himself. His small empire is a detached building, having seen better days, set in rural Essex, alongside a disused foundry. Nearby runs a watery creek and two enormously tall trees. How very peaceful.

But not quite the small publisher I was hoping for. I expected sleek offices in a tall Georgian building somewhere near Bath. At the very least.

Nevertheless, the meeting goes well. Samuel Spink of Spink and Ffitch Publications loves the book. A few minor changes are suggested - a couple of chapters cut, different title, some character alterations, nothing I can't handle. I point out my book is based on a true crime and therefore needs little embellishment. But Mr Spink sets me straight. Market forces and all that.

After many phone calls and much rewriting I leave the final proof reading to the publisher. I do have a small reservation - not too keen on the new title. My book, 'Dirty Moonlight'- a true tale of smuggling and murder, is now called, 'The Body in the Cellar'- a sensational story of blood, lust and revenge.

Finally, I receive the proof copy. A momentous day, only slightly marred by the fact that I have some trouble recognising my own work.

The cover, which I had visualised in monochrome, showing a muddy night sky above still dark water with a quaint fishing inn in the foreground, has now a blood red background with a solitary candle lighting a gruesome corpse hanging from a rusty net hook.

Some parts of the text are tricky to identify too. It's amazing how a slight adjustment can make such a vast difference. Too late now. Publish and be damned!

The book is a great success. We're in the middle of a second run: it's above John Grisham in the local bookshop's chart this week. I'm being asked for a sequel and nameless people are talking about a TV film. I'm over the moon………….until I hear who they have in mind for the main roles.

For the plain servant girl they want Amanda Holden. The smuggler with a social conscience, John Leslie and, scariest of all, for the ageing but charismatic Lord of the Manor, hiding a bitter inheritance, they're in talks with Ricky Tomlinson.

I have decided upon early retirement. Away to a little cottage on the South coast of Scotland, bought with my ill written gains. And, I think, to seek out the local writer's group.

A Cautionary Tale

Greedy Peter had a bun
Greedy Rita wanted some
Rita tried to grab the cake
But she made a huge mistake
Peter and Rita fought and fought
A lesson they would soon be taught
They lost their hold, they dropped the bun
Peter and Rita then had none

by Natalie Hudson

Sordid Soap
by SJ Banham

"Do I know you?" Annie asked softly, almost clumsily. She stood patiently in the queue behind the man, glancing up at his height. He must have easily been over six feet. She studied his dark brown hair, hand-combed backwards. It looked as if it had been allowed to grow out from a style. It curled slightly at the edges and one side was tucked behind his ear. From this angle she could see a mole on his left jaw just underneath his ear lobe. "I'm sorry," she continued, "I'm sure I know you."

The young man smiled but shook his head.

"I don't think so."

"I do know you, I'm sure of it. I never forget a face you see. Names," she chuckled, "now they're a different story."

He turned to face her again. His denim jacked brought out the blue in his eyes. It was as if she had seen him in a dream, as if he had been part of a distant memory.

"I'm sorry, but would you mind telling me your name? It might make a difference." She blushed as her brown hair swayed gently on her twenty-five year old shoulders. Standing in a shopping line with a bottle of washing up liquid in her hands interrogating the other customers wasn't exactly what she had in mind when she awoke this morning. But here she was.

"I'm Annie Scott," she added by way of a softener. It was her intention to sound friendly not freakish.

The man nodded, extended an uneasy handshake whilst holding a packet of four toilet tissues in cornflower blue, and smiled at her.

"Hello Annie Scott," he smiled. "I'm Glynn Harper."

"No," she shook her head slowly with confusion. "That's not it."

Glynn laughed, catching the attention of the other customers in the queue.

"Yeah," he told her. "It is."

"No, you just don't look like a Glynn. I'd go with a Michael, Mick, Mickey, that kind of name."

"Sorry," he continued smiling, unable to see past her cheekiness. "It's definitely Glynn. Maybe I look like someone you know."

"Yeah, you do," she laughed. "You!"

"No, I meant like your boyfriend?"

Annie tilted her head. He was flirting with her.

"I know it isn't that because I don't have one. Look, sorry, you must think I'm some kind of weirdo but I definitely know you but not by that name. Do you have a twin?"

Glimpsing at the other customers, some of whom were smiling equally as hard and others who just didn't care whether she knew him or not, Glynn moved up the queue.

"Nope. I don't know what to tell you, maybe we knew each other in another life." He hadn't meant it to sound quite so flirtatious, but by the look on Annie's face, she hadn't minded in the least.

"I don't believe in that stuff."

"Just because you don't believe in something doesn't make it impossible." He told her.

"Tell me, did you ever work in Selfridges? I worked there for a little while a few years ago. Maybe it was there."

The look on his face told her it wasn't there.

"I'll let you into a little secret, Annie," Glynn said, "I'm new to London. I just moved here a week ago." He looked down at his single shopping item. "Hence the toilet roll. I forgot to get some. Remembered coffee, sugar and just about every type of cleaning product known to man but loo rolls? Nope." He gestured to his head. "Losing it, I reckon. My age I suppose."

Annie laughed. He was thirty if he was a day. But at least he was talking to her. She had hoped he didn't think she was some loon but he seemed fairly happy to chat. Maybe if he continued, she could place him.

"Where did you move from?"

"I was working abroad, thought I'd stop a while in the city."

"So, if it isn't Selfridges then," she went on, "Where could it have been?"

"Sorry, can't help you." He moved further up the queue and she moved up behind him.

"You're not a model are you?" she asked before her brain could tell her mouth not to. "I'm sorry, it does sound awfully personal, but you are, you know, fairly good looking, in a sort of male-model kind of way." She cursed herself as she got herself deeper and deeper into trouble. "I didn't mean that to sound insulting, sorry!"

Glynn laughed aloud, this time catching more attention from other shoppers.

"Only fairly good-looking?" he asked trying not to burst into laughter. Annie was already a beetroot colour from her last question, she didn't need to turn entirely maroon. "No, sorry. I'm not, neither have I ever been, a male-model."

He turned back just in time to have the shop assistant scan his item. He paid, bagged the toilet rolls and shot Annie a grin and a wave.

"Nice to have chatted, Annie, maybe I'll see you around?"

She watched him leave as the assistant scanned her washing up liquid. It would come to her eventually, she told herself as she left the shop. Walking towards Leicester Square from Piccadilly Circus, she unconsciously looked ahead and across the road. Suddenly someone appeared beside her.

"Hi again, Annie." It was him. Grinning like a Cheshire cat, he walked with her. "I had a feeling I'd see you around."

"So are you going to tell me where I know you from or are you going to keep me in suspense?"

"Truly, I haven't got a clue." He winked, then said theatrically, "though I do have a terribly murky and distant past." He pulled his jacket over his face which revealed nothing but his eyes. His tease hadn't helped a bit. She just wanted to know more than before now.

"And this murky and distant past would be the reason why you moved to London, yes?" she tested.

"Possibly." He narrowed his eyes and raised an eyebrow, continuing the tease.

"This is driving me nuts!" she squealed with frustration. "Where could we possibly have met? I've never so much as set foot outside this country and you've only just arrived in London?"

"Don't think about it, and it will come to you. Meanwhile," he asked boldly, "can I buy you a coffee?"

She stared up at him. What was the worst that could happen? They were in a public place and she had instigated the conversation.

"Sure," she agreed. "Why not?"

Thirty minutes of idly chatting over coffee later, two middle aged men pushed through the entrance to the coffee shop. Glynn saw them instantly and turned an insipid pink colour.

"Uh, Annie." She turned around to see what had frightened him but he pulled her back quickly to face him. "I, uh, I've got to go. I'm sorry!"

She stood after him and grabbed hold of her jacket. "What's the matter? Shall I come with you?"

Before he had a chance to answer her, he was walking quickly out towards the back of the shop. Annie followed blindly leaving their shopping on the seats.

"Glynn! Wait! What's going on?"

He stopped and steered into a room at the back of the shop grabbing her close to him. Holding her in front of him with a hand over her mouth, he opened the door a crack to see if the men were approaching. They didn't appear to be. He closed the door quietly. She looked up at him with inquisitive eyes as he released his hand.

"What the hell's going on?" she stage-whispered, hoping like hell the place she had seen him before wasn't on a 'wanted' poster at the local underground. "Are you in some kind of trouble?"

"It's complicated."

"Well, I'm all ears."

"Annie, I'm sorry. I can't explain right now. I've got to get out of here. I had no idea they'd come looking for me here!"

"Who? Who's after you?"

"I can't talk about it. I'm sorry." He looked around the room for a telephone but, other than boxes from floor to ceiling filled with coffee beans, there was nothing. "I have to make a phone call. Do you have a phone I could use?"

She took out her mobile and offered it to him and just as she did so, she had a rush of memory. He was an actor, the star of a new soap early last year. He was to be the 'bad-boy'. She'd read about him in the papers shortly after it had begun. He'd been replaced almost before it had started, something about him going into hiding after witnessing something highly dodgy. He'd been given no choice but to give up his career on the screen.

"It's not Glynn Harper, is it?" she asked sympathetically. "I know who you are now."

He dialled a number and turned away from her.

"Witness Protection?" he said softly. "Giles Pennyworth please. Mickey Stanford here. I'm in deep trouble. I think they've found me."

The Spring of '45

The Union Jack so proudly shown,
Distracted from the street,
The bombed out shells that once were home,
To folk I'd never meet.

Street parties came with tables laid,
We danced and sang for more.
What was this peace for which we'd prayed,
I'd known nothing else but war.

A little girl with a pink dress on,
With ribbons in my hair,
Too young to know why we'd fought so long,
With a man no longer there.

Pictures of him were placed at night,
On a bonfire along the drive.
I watched them burn in the twisted light,
In the Spring of '45.

by Sis Unsworth

A Model Son
by G K Harris

Davey Clark watched the plane circling around him, the buzz of its engine music in his ears.

"This is great fun dad," he said, his grin broadening across his pale cheeks. His father was watching as well, but with a more concerned eye, as the wind suddenly came in strong across the cliff top. In the fading light, Davey hadn't seen the trees further along its edge bowing to its strength.

His eyes were on only one thing, following it like target lasers.

"Keep a tight hold on that line Davey and pull it in to you, in case that gust catches it." Davey laughed, almost hysterically.

"Don't worry, dad, I've got the hang of it now." But his joy quickly turned to horror, as the control lines of his small scale model aircraft pulled hard in his hand. He tried to make the correction, but it was all too quickly lifted, as it turned towards the shimmering waves, the gust flipping it over into a looping nose dive. Davey put a hand over his eyes, his imagination answering all his fears for him as he felt the line go slack, the sound of shattering balsa wood and dope hardened paper hitting the ground hard now filling his ears. Davey sensed his father wince, then run to where his plane had made its unscheduled and untidy landing.

"It's all right, Davey, it's only the wing that shattered!" Davey dropped the control line and ran to where his father stood, and eyed the wreckage of his plane with a sad intensity. He bent down and picked it up, holding its body in one hand and its shattered wing in the other. His father smiled at him, then took the wing and held it up to inspect it more closely. Then he laughed. Davey didn't, he was trying to look grown up about it, but he knew what he really wanted to do.

"It's OK, son." He felt his father nudge him in the shoulder. "It's not the end of the world, it's only the wing, we can soon rebuild it." His father pointed. "Look, the fuselage is intact. With a new wing and propeller, it'll soon fly again, you'll see." Davey forced a smile. "That's the spirit son."

His father's words echoed in his ears as they walked back through the thick grass that covered the crest of the cliff where he and his father met at the place where they had always come, to fly his plane.

The light was fading fast now. "Do you have to go, dad?" Davey looked at him with eyes deep and round, as he waited for his answer.

"I'm afraid I must, Davey, I have to go back." Davey watched his father's image beginning to grow weak in the poor light as it began to lay the cliffs and fields around them slowly to rest. He knew his dad loved him and would always come back to meet him and fly his planes with him. But he wanted to be with his dad forever.

Davey knew by the look in his father's eye that he knew what he was thinking. And what his father was going to say, he knew was right, and for the best.

"It's best if your mother doesn't know about me coming here and us meeting like this. I don't think she would understand, and besides it would only upset her to know."

Davey wanted to put his arms around his father and hug him,

but he knew he couldn't.

"It's OK, dad, I'm sure she'll get over it one day." Davey had been close to his father right from when he could first remember. It was his father's interest in model aeroplanes that got him started flying them himself. Sometimes his mother wouldn't see them all day, because they were either in the shed building and repairing them, or on the cliff top flying them. Davey remembered the only day his mother had ever come with them. He knew she wasn't really that interested and she didn't like the thought of them on the cliff top either, but with his father's help he managed to persuade her, because it was going to be the first time his dad was going to fly a remote control plane.

Davey remembered his excitement when they got there, and how he ran about all over the place, chasing after the plane.

"Don't go dad, do you remember that day you flew that big spitfire, the one that flew on its own, that was something to watch wasn't it?" His father was getting fainter, and tears began to moisten his eyes.

"I've tried to forget that plane, Davey," he said. "It caused so much pain for your mother, it's best left where it is." It was obvious that both father and son did not want to part.

"You must go, Davey, your mother will be waiting at home."

"You will come again, won't you, dad, perhaps mum would like to come too, like she did that day when you had to climb down the cliff to get the plane, I'm sure she'd understand if she did."

His father's head shook sombrely. "No, Davey, she must never come: it would be too much for her to see us together like this." Davey's eyes filled with sadness as his father's image was now almost nothing, now that the sky around him filled with a soft, glowing light, that he knew would soon be getting brighter. He knew it was time to say goodbye to his father until next time, and that there was nothing he could do to stop it in the end.

But, the bond between them was as strong as ever, even after all these years, and it was still holding them together. Davey also knew that if their love for each other ever faded, then so would his father's memory.

Davey waved as the car drove away and he was all alone again still holding his broken plane. He held it up and thought of what his father had said to him after it had crashed. Yes there are things you can repair, he thought, like this old plane you built for me a long time ago, but then there are things you can't. You would have fixed that spitfire, but you couldn't. Davey walked back across the field to the cliff top, the light around him getting brighter all the while. Then as he stood on its crumbling edge, it beckoned, almost called to him. He turned.

"We'll always fly this plane together though, dad, he said. Broken bodies are hard to fix though aren't they dad, he thought. Still I don't blame you, dad, and I'm sure mum doesn't either, after all, I was very excited, and it was quite slippery that day I fell, wasn't it?"

Then he stepped over the edge and into the light with both its wings like new.

Melanie

Once we walked on Paulin's strand
when you when here with me,
and as we progressed hand in hand
by glittering sea and golden sand,
we found a new born virgin land,
when you were here with me

And there we built a castle tall
when you were here with me,
of sand and shells and dreams and all,
with lofty tower and stately hall,
a fortress that could never fall,
when you were here with me.

But soon the gods in jealous spite,
when you were here with me,
to gratify cruel appetite
did stir the clouds and dim the light
and all our fancies put to flight,
and then you turned from me.

And now the greedy ocean's wave,
when you are far from me,
claws back the land that once it gave
and fleeting joys and castles brave
like childhood's toys I ere must save,
till you come back to me.

cont >

And we will walk on Paulin's shore
when you return to me,
and all that magic land explore
as hand in hand we go once more
and you will love me as before,
When you come home to me.

By Peter Freeman

I Want to Look into Your Eyes

I want to look into your eyes
To lose myself in their intensity and beauty
To hold you and never have to let go
To feel you, above me, beneath me, within me
Right to the very core of my being
To lay with you just watching, feeling
Believing nothing could be wrong while you are there.
Thinking I could take on the world
As long as I have you by my side
I want to care for you
To cherish and comfort you
To make you feel as invincible as I do
When I'm around you
To inhale your scent, to feel your warmth
And to know that you'll always be there

by Natalie Hudson

Fly on a Diet
by Bernice Bedford

Ageing is news yet again. Or more precisely, avoiding the ageing process and finding eternal youth. Diets, nips, tucks, botox, detox, face-lifts. The stress of finding your way through the anti-stress, anti-ageing products is considerable.

Even death need no longer be the end. In America a handful of very rich, very old men are on ice waiting to be defrosted when the time is right. Apparently it would work more successfully if you were frozen before death. But how do you choose when to go? At your peak? On your decline? When someone buys you a copy of The Oldie?

But, you may ask, is this where the painful growth of civilisation intended to lead us? All the great thinkers, engineers, peacemakers; were they just paving the way to enable us to thaw out elderly people like so many fish fingers? Did Edwardian women chain themselves to the railings only for us to be chained to our plastic surgeons?

Perhaps we should look towards more humble beings. Did you know that lobsters never age? Apparently a twenty-year old lobster looks exactly like a two year old one. This is pretty hard to prove, of course, as most lobsters are caught and eaten before their teens. But I like to imagine a solitary scientist on a remote island, closely monitoring a colony of elderly lobsters, happily running amok in salt water tanks, forever young and beautiful.

Maybe therapists should chat to the worm. A mildly stressed

worm will live longer than a worm without a care in the world. Chill out is not necessarily cool in worm talk.

And life expectancy for fruit flies will be noticeably shortened if they reproduce too often. Many women can identify with them.

Other flies die younger if they eat too much. Mother Nature can be very cruel indeed. Such abundance of choice needs so much restraint. A fly on a diet will have many more days hovering around crap as long as he does not indulge. How unfair is that? Where's the fun in a life without excreta?

The good news is that the latest media frenzy is for maintaining a youthful brain. You may find this a little OTT. But consider, what use a fine, unlined supple body teamed with an ancient brain? What is the point of being fit enough to salsa all night if you cannot remember the steps? And most important of all - this diet actually includes all the food we love - red wine, strawberries, smoked salmon and chocolate. Not only a diet of everything divine but no cooking involved. You can use all the kitchen time saved, for sitting and thinking with your agile and youthful brain. I have waited all my life for a diet like this and it is so much better than being a mildly stressed worm.

So here's to laughter lines, low slung boobs, greying hair, and a brain fresh and young as a child's. My daughter says I have begun the process already.

The Queue
by Peter Freeman and Sis Unsworth

Lizzie stared into her cupboard.

"Not much left of the rations," she thought. Still there was only herself and little Molly to feed, what with Jim being away in the army. Her thoughts were interrupted by her sister, Jean, calling from the landing below.

"Lizzie, 'urry up! There's a queue forming at Sid's. Someone said oranges!"

"All right, I'm coming," Lizzie replied, scooping up Molly with one hand and poking back the lock of hair that had escaped from her turban with the other and headed for the door.

At the front of the concrete tenement stairs, Lizzie put the sleepy Molly into her battered pushchair, whilst Jean exchanged a few friendly words with Mrs Lehman, who was busy scrubbing her step.

"Ain't she coming?" Lizzie inquired when they were out of earshot.

"Nar, not even Adolph Hitler could stop 'er from cleaning that step on a Monday morning," Jean replied, and the sisters giggled as they pushed Molly towards the queue.

"Funny old wevver for September, ain't it? Not very cheerful," remarked Jean as they hurried along. When they reached the end of the queue they met Doll, a neighbour; all peroxide and painted nails.

"What's the queue for Doll, is it oranges?" Lizzie asked.

"I think so," came the amiable reply. "Five years this bloody war's been going on and nowadays whenever I see a queue, I gets on the end of it."

"It's the bleeding shortages I can't cope with," said Lizzie as she placed a dummy in Molly's mouth and gently rocked the pushchair.

A group of children, in hand-me-down clothes and ill fitting shoes, played hopscotch in the street nearby; their shouts of excitement rivalling the chatter of the growing queue.

"If this war goes on much longer, them kids down there'll forget what their farvers looked like, them as knew who they were, that is!" Lizzie said with a shake of her head.

Just then, a hush came over the queue. One by one they turned to stare at the bottom of the street. Lizzie stopped rocking the push chair, ignoring the lock of hair that had escaped again and followed the gaze of her sister. Something more feared than the bombs had entered the small world of Whitecross Street, with its population of anxious mothers, and potential widows. A telegram boy, complete with Post Office bike, had appeared and had apparently stopped to ask Mrs Lehman for directions. Drying her hands on her pinafore, she stood up painfully, turned and pointed in the direction of the silent apprehensive queue where the noisy game of hopscotch was now unheeded.

From the distance came the sound of an accelerating motor and the strident, insistent sound of a jangling bell. In that other world, removed from the queue and the telegram boy, the every day life of the East End was going on as usual. The ambulance, or was it a police car, pursued its urgent business.

Nearby, a man was singing in Italian as he helped to clear away the rubble from a bombed-out house. It sounded like opera, but no-one in that fearful line would afterwards remember hearing a sound.

The telegram boy was a lanky pimply youth who had grown out of his uniform. As he approached thirty pairs of eyes took in every aspect of his appearance. He had covered about two thirds of the distance, and Lizzie's grip on Jean's arm had become painfully tight, when suddenly Lizzie found herself flying, with empty lungs and screaming senses, across the road and hard into a wall.

When eventually she awoke in hospital, her first thoughts were for Molly and Jean.

"Just cuts and bruises," the Irish nurse told her. "They're doing fine." And so she slept for a while and the sleep gave back her strength.

When next she awoke, Jean was beside the bed holding her good hand. The other, she found, sported a broken wrist and was splinted and plastered.

"You back wiv us then?" said Jean cheerfully.

"I couldn't 'alf do wiv a cuppa," replied Lizzie, forcing her damaged face to return Jean's relieved smile.

Later, enveloped in a borrowed pink dressing-gown which was several sizes too big, and painfully sipping her tea, she began to ask questions. Hushing her sister with a raised hand and taking a deep breath, Jean began.

"Molly is fine, luv, and Mrs Lehman is treating her like a film star. She's been wonderful, Mrs Lehman 'as, couldn't do enough for us that woman. She's been looking after Molly since you came in 'ere. Doctor says she only has cuts and bruises like me, so Mrs Lehman took 'er 'ome. They reckon the explosion was caused by a gas main going up, but I don't fink it was. I reckon it was some kind of bomb meself. Stands to reason. That bus driver in the top flat, you know 'im what keeps banging the door, well 'e says there was one in Stratford and two in Leyton on the same day. Funny fing, the only one to get killed down our road was that telegram boy. 'e was caught in the open see. They say the bang went off in Falmouth Road, the uvver side of them big 'ouses. There was a lot copped it over there, but you was the only one of us lot to be kept in 'ere over night. 'e was going to the next block up the street Mrs Lehman says, you know, that telegram boy, so it wasn't for us at all. So my Wally's probably all right." Then hurriedly, "An' your Jim an' all, o'course."

Jean paused for a mouthful of tea and Lizzie pounced on the opportunity to speak.

"What's the flat like then?"

Jean parried at the question.

"Well, you'll 'ave to 'ave new windows and that, but keep your chin up luv, worse fings 'appen at sea, and it ain't that bad, honest."

"Well that's as maybe, Jeanie Bennet," said Lizzie with a shake of her head, "but I bet Ma Lehman ain't too 'appy, what wiv 'er 'aving to do the step twice in the one week, and what's more, we never did get our 'ands on the them bleeding oranges, did we!"

Ghosts versus Goolies
by Myra Baxter

The power of goolies is great. Their power can be used for good or evil. When used with good intent, in the manner in which nature intended, they give birth to great joy. However, used indiscriminately they cause havoc.

Ghosts, on the other hand, can be comforting and charismatic. They have been undeservedly labelled as scary. Personally I have never encountered a frightening ghost. Some ghosts, when they appear, look just as they did in life. These are very friendly. Other ghosts seem to enjoy floating about in the mist. They mean no harm. Occasionally one may pop up unexpectedly and surprise someone. This, of course, can be disconcerting but rarely causes any real damage. At such times the air has been known to turn blue.

Why people shudder at the mere mention of ghosts I do not know. Goolies, on the other hand, should be regarded as dangerous, particularly by young and attractive women. Some older ladies cannot afford to be complacent, needing to remember that there are goolies about. While ghosts will appear to either sex, goolies prefer to parade their powers before females.

Ghosts do not intentionally harm anyone. They are not to

blame if the sight of them causes panic. Goolies, however, can be a threat and should be handled with care. Their eagerness to display their prowess can cause distress. Their ability to demonstrate their skills, without the least encouragement, becomes abundantly evident. They are prepared to go to great lengths to impress even complete strangers.

To sum up - it is seldom one sees a ghost, whereas goolies abound. It is the living who are to be feared, not the ghosts.

I rest my case.

The Meaning of Us

You make me happy
You make me smile
When you're around
Life seems more worthwhile
When you are with me
Skies never seem grey
Just hearing your voice
Brightens up my day
You cheer me up
When I'm feeling bad
You make me realise
Things aren't so bad
Now I've written this poem
So you know that it's true
Just how much you mean to me
And how much I love you

By Natalie Hudson

Out There
by Myra Baxter

As I stood gazing out to the far horizon, the hills at my back, I heard the curlew call. Again and again it called. There was magic in that sound. It spoke to me of indescribable beauty and freedom from the constraints of human existence. It reached my spirit, sending it high on wings of wonder. In that moment I was at one with earth, sea and sky. I belonged. It surely happened. Eternity did not seem unthinkable any more. The curlew, I felt sure, had knowledge of matters beyond human comprehension.

When the need to escape the mundane drives me back to the wild places, I wait in stillness. Nature embraces me. I am assured that this is my spiritual home. The magic flows around me and in me. I rejoice. Summer and Winter that call can be heard - out there.